LETTERS,
PRINCIPAL DOCTRINES,
AND
VATICAN SAYINGS

The Library of Liberal Arts
OSKAR PIEST, FOUNDER

LETTERS
PRINCIPAL DOCTRINES
AND
VATICAN SAYINGS

EPICURUS

Translated, with an Introduction and Notes, by
RUSSEL M. GEER

· ·

The Library of Liberal Arts
published by

Macmillan Publishing Company
New York
Collier Macmillan Publishers
London

Epicurus: *c.* 341 - 271 B.C.

• • • • • • • • • • • • • • • • • • • •

First Edition
Nineteenth Printing — 1988

Library of Congress Catalog Card Number: 61-18059
ISBN 0-02-341200-3

PREFACE

In preparing this translation of the chief extant works of Epicurus, my effort has been first to discover as exactly as possible the meaning of a passage, and then to express that meaning in readily understandable English. As anyone who has struggled with Epicurus' Greek will know, this has forced me to use very great freedom in rendering the text; and in many places what I have presented is not so much a translation as a paraphrase. The notes are intended to give to the nonclassical reader the information that he may need for an understanding of the Epicurean material. There is very little here that is new, but most of it has been buried in commentaries not easily usable by anyone without a ready command of Greek and Latin.

The present work was originally intended to appear in a single volume with a similar annotated translation of the poem *On Nature,* in which the Roman poet, Lucretius, has given us what is the fullest treatment of Epicurean physical theories now extant; but it has seemed wiser to publish the two translations separately. Since, however, the companion volume will appear soon after this one, the many cross references to Lucretius in the commentary have been allowed to stand, for in very many places Lucretius' longer discussions furnish us the best aid we have for understanding the highly compressed presentation in Epicurus.

In general, I have followed Bailey's text, but I have adopted a few readings from von der Muehll, and in a few instances I have retained conjectures by Usener that Bailey rejected. (For these and other editions, see the Bibliography, page xxxix.) I have received constant aid from Bailey's translation and from his commentary, and somewhat less assistance from the translation by Hicks in the Loeb Classical Library. In a few cases, usually where I have translated a different text, I have

quoted one or both of these translations in my notes. For
permission to do this I thank the Oxford University Press and
the Harvard University Press.

Most of the work on this volume was done during summer
vacations with books borrowed from the library of Bowdoin
College in Brunswick, Maine; and I wish again as on several
past occasions to thank the staff of that library for their unfailing generosity and courtesy.

Except for the *Vatican Sayings,* all the material here translated is from Book Ten of Diogenes Laertius' *Lives of the
Philosophers.* The sections (appearing as marginal numbers)
into which this was divided by early editors are quite arbitrary with little or no relation to any logical division of the
subject matter. In order to retain the traditional numbering
and at the same time make exact cross references possible I
have often divided the sections, e.g., 31a, 31b, or 38a, 38b, 38c.
In the *Letters* I have also made divisions into chapters, sections, and at times subsections, with titles and summaries to
each. These are not found in the original, and the summaries
are printed in italic type to distinguish them from the actual
text. Longer notes and commentary will be found in the Appendix, pp. 75-89.

RUSSEL M. GEER

CONTENTS

INTRODUCTION

I. The Period Before Epicurus

SOURCES OF OUR KNOWLEDGE OF THE
EARLY GREEK PHYSICAL THEORIES

Our best evidence for the ancient atomic explanation [a] of
the universe is Lucretius' poem *On Nature,* which has come
down to us as he left it at his death, lacking the final touches
but virtually complete. He makes no claim to originality;
rather, he constantly proclaims his debt to Epicurus. Of Epicurus' own voluminous works we possess, aside from brief
passages quoted by other writers in works that are extant, only
the three epitomes in the form of letters and the forty *Principal Doctrines,* included by Diogenes Laertius in the account
of Epicurus that forms the last book of his *Lives of the Philosophers.* Although Epicurus himself claimed complete originality and denied any debt whatever to any thinkers before
himself, it is perfectly clear that his system of physics was
borrowed with some changes—which are not always improvements—from that developed by Leucippus and Democritus,
behind which lies a long line of development reaching back
at least to Thales. Of the men responsible for this development, all but Thales and possibly Heraclitus wrote books;
however, only scattered fragments of these remain, embedded
in the works of others. For example, of the writings of Anaximander we have five fragments totaling about seven lines;
of those of Democritus we have nearly three hundred fragments, the longest of them containing about twenty-five lines,
but many consisting of only a few words and most of them
dealing with ethics rather than with physics. Also important

[a] For this and all subsequent references indicated by superior letters,
see Appendix, pp. 75-89.

for our understanding of these early physicists or philosophers are the statements about them and their beliefs made by others. Unfortunately, one ancient philosopher usually referred to another only to disagree with him. Thus Lucretius, in his long discussion of Anaxagoras (I. 830-920), far from trying to understand and explain his actual beliefs, states them baldly, or rather misstates them, and then goes on to prove that, assuming the truth of his own atomic theory, the earlier theory is false. In the same way Aristotle, who often prefaced his own theories about the natural world with a summary of earlier beliefs, regarded all physical and cosmological theories before his own as clumsy and vain efforts toward the truth; his discussions of his predecessors are regularly expressed in terms of his own theories and are far from being sympathetic or understanding. Unfortunately, this seems also to have been the attitude of Theophrastus, one of Aristotle's immediate successors, whose great *History of Philosophy*, now lost, is the ultimate source of most of the later comment on Democritus and his predecessors.

THALES AND THE BEGINNING OF GREEK PHYSICAL PHILOSOPHY [1]

Greek efforts to explain the world in rational rather than mythological terms begin, at least for us, with Thales of Miletus (fl. *c.* 585 B.C.). Many stories, a few of which may be true, are told of his activity as a practical man of affairs, a traveler, statesman, engineer, and mathematician. That he foretold a solar eclipse in 585 B.C. is important chiefly in fixing his own date, since he certainly did not understand the nature of the phenomenon and was simply using tables that had been compiled in Babylon. We need concern ourselves only with his statement that all things are formed from water.

1 For Thales, see C. Bailey, *Greek Atomists and Epicurus* (Oxford, 1928), pp. 12-13 (unless otherwise indicated, references to Bailey in this Introduction will be to his *Atomists*); J. Burnet, *Early Greek Philosophy* (4th edn.; London, 1930), pp. 39-50; G. S. Kirk and J. E. Raven, *Presocratic Philosophers* (Cambridge, England, 1957), pp. 74-98.

We do not know what led him to this belief. Aristotle is clearly guessing when he says that it was because water is needed for all forms of life, and we ourselves may with equal right conjecture that it was because water is the only common substance that exists in nature as solid, liquid, and vapor. Nor do we know quite what his statement meant. Is water a permanent basic substance from which the objects that we recognize with the senses are temporarily formed and into which they return? Or is water simply something necessary for all birth and growth and nothing more than that?

ANAXIMANDER [2]

We do know, however, that Anaximander (fl. *c.* 570 B.C.), a fellow citizen of Thales and somewhat younger, sought a basic substance from which all things, including our world [3] in all its parts, are formed and into which they will all pass when they are destroyed. This substance he called the *apeiron,* the "unlimited" or "undefined." By this we may understand that it was unlimited quantitatively—that is, it was spatially infinite so that matter for creation might not fail—and also that it was undefined qualitatively—that is, it had no qualities of its own lest, being infinite, it make all things like itself.

Some ancient sources attribute to Anaximander a belief that our world is one of many. This has been doubted, but his explanation of the formation of our world is compatible with such a belief. A portion of the *apeiron* separated from the rest, then divided into two opposites, the hot (including air and

[2] For Anaximander, see Bailey, pp. 14-16; Burnet, pp. 50-71; Kirk and Raven, pp. 99-142.

[3] The term "world" will regularly be used to indicate an earth more or less like ours and the celestial bodies that appear to move about it. The possibility of many such worlds was recognized by many ancient thinkers. "Earth" will be used to designate that which is under our feet and about which the celestial bodies seem to revolve; and "universe" will mean all that exists and, in the case of those philosophers who recognize it, the void in which matter exists and through which it moves.

fire) and the cold (including earth and water).[4] The cold gathered together at the center and became the earth with its land and its seas, rivers, and lakes, the whole shaped like a column drum whose upper side is the earth's surface as we know it, three times as broad as it is deep, remaining at rest because it is in the center. The hot gathered together outside the cold and then divided into a large number of rings of varying diameters that circle the earth, turning on an axis, not parallel to the earth's surface as we see it but running through the pole star and some opposite point below the earth.[5] Each ring is a hollow tube with fire on the inside and opaque air on the surface, and each is provided with one opening through which the fire shines out as a heavenly body.[6] The largest ring, that of the sun, has a diameter twenty-seven (or twenty-eight) times the diameter of the earth, and the aperture through which the fire shines is as large as the earth. The ring of the moon is eighteen times the earth's diameter, and the rings of the stars and planets have lesser diameters and presumably are narrower, since the fires that they show are smaller. In the sources, there is no mention of the motion of the sun between its summer and winter courses in the sky

[4] The four elements—earth, air, fire, and water—first become important in the system of Empedocles (pp. xviii ff. below), but they run through all Greek thinking before and after him. They are certainly present here, and atomists like Epicurus and Lucretius, who denied their existence as elements, often found it convenient to explain phenomena in terms of the four.

[5] That all the rings revolve about such an axis is not stated in our scanty sources, but it is necessary if the phenomena are to be explained. We are told that the rings are of different diameters—the diameters of the rings of sun and moon being given, but not those of the stars—and that the ring of the moon is oblique. I find no authority whatever for Kirk's statement (Kirk and Raven, pp. 136-37) that the rings of all the stars are of the same size; and it would be almost impossible to visualize the motions of the stars near the pole on any such supposition.

[6] Kirk suggests that the "air" of these rings has the property of the air in Homer, which is used by the gods to conceal a hero, and which makes the hero transparent like itself. Thus the sun, most distant from the earth, would be visible through the lesser rings.

or of its annual progression through the zodiac, nor is there any mention of the similar motions of the moon and the planets. Since these motions, or at least those of the sun and moon, were well known, it is probable that some explanation was given, perhaps winds blowing in various directions at various times. However, it does not appear likely that Anaximander gave any explanation for motion itself, either the original separation of the opposites and the formation of the world or the continuing motions of the celestial bodies. If he felt that no explanation of motion was needed, he was in this respect like the other early physicists. It was only after Parmenides that this was recognized as an important problem.

All through antiquity it was believed that certain of the simplest forms of animal life might be generated directly from warm mud.[7] Anaximander believed that in this same way the first life on earth was produced spontaneously at the edge of the sea. These earliest creatures lived in the water, and from them land animals gradually evolved. Since of all living creatures man has the longest childhood during which he is dependent on others, the first generations of men must, believed Anaximander, have been formed in large sharklike fish and sent forth into the struggle of life only when strong enough to maintain themselves.

ANAXIMENES [8]

Of the life of Anaximenes (fl. 546 B.C.) we know only that he was a little younger than Anaximander and like him a native of Miletus. Anaximander had stripped his basic substance of all qualities. Anaximenes found a way in which quantity could account for differences in quality. His basic substance is air, and in its normal state it possesses the properties of air. It is infinite in extent, as was the *apeiron*. As air condenses and becomes more compact, it first becomes mist;

[7] See Lucretius, II. 871-73.

[8] For Anaximenes, see Bailey, pp. 16-18; Burnet, pp. 72-79; Kirk and Raven, pp. 143-62.

then as the process continues it changes successively into water, earth, and the harder substances. By rarefaction it returns through the various stages and becomes air once more; and if the rarefaction continues fire is formed. If the air that had filled a room were so condensed that it occupied a few cubic inches, we could well believe that its qualities would change—that it might assume the form of a rock. Conversely, if the matter in a pebble were so rarefied that it filled a large room, it might become what our senses recognize as air. We are here on the verge of an atomic system, but with Anaximenes the matter is thought of as being continuous, not as being made up of minute moving particles which are themselves unchanging and which are separated from each other by varying amounts of empty space.

Of Anaximenes' cosmology little is known. The earth was formed by the condensation of part of the infinite air; and the heavenly bodies were in turn formed by mist that rose from the earth and became rarefied into fire. The earth itself is a flat disk resting on air; the sun and moon do not pass below the earth but rather go around its northern edge, hidden from our eyes by higher land to the north. We shall find that Epicurus, whose weakest point is astronomy, does not reject this theory.[9] The question of the causes of the original condensation by which the earth was formed and of the condensation and rarefaction that is constantly going on about us seems not to have been raised by Anaximenes, just as the similar question was ignored by Anaximander.

XENOPHANES [10]

Xenophanes, whose long life may have extended from *c.* 570 to *c.* 475, was born in Colophon in Ionia but lived chiefly in the Greek-speaking parts of Italy and Sicily. We have more than one hundred scattered lines, including two fragments of about twenty-five lines each, from the poems in which he

9 Epicurus, *Letter to Pythocles* 92. Cf. Aristotle, *Meteorology* B. 1, 354 a 28.

10 For Xenophanes, see Burnet, pp. 112-29; Kirk and Raven, pp. 163-81.

expressed his opinions in regard to gods, men, and the world in general. Some of them, or perhaps all, went under the name *Silloi,* "Satires." The longest fragments are little to our present purpose. Best known of them are the several groups of verses in which he attacks the anthropomorphic gods of Homer and Hesiod. In one, for example, he says: "If oxen, horses, and lions had hands and could paint and make statues as do men, the horses would picture their gods like horses, the oxen like oxen, and they would each give to their gods bodies like their own." [11] If he wrote a separate work on nature, little or nothing of it survives. The opinions on cosmology ascribed to him seem to come from poems in which he is trying to explain phenomena without bringing in the gods. Thus the sun is formed of little sparks of fire collected from the mist that rose from the sea, or again, it is an ignited cloud. This last explanation is also given for the moon, the rainbow, and the stars. There are many suns and moons for different regions of the earth. We see a new sun each morning. The sun at night does not go beneath the earth but moves off to infinity, seeming to move in a curved path because of the increasing distance. The attitude of Xenophanes toward astronomy seems much like that of Epicurus, and we may conjecture that both had the same purpose. They wrote not trying to present a consistent cosmology but only to show that gods, at least gods of the Homeric type, were not needed to explain what we see in the air above us. One striking use of evidence should, however, be noted. It had been held by others, both mythmakers and philosophers, that the sea had once covered the land; but Xenophanes may have been the first to cite as proof of this fossils of fish and seaweed found far inland.

HERACLITUS [12]

Heraclitus of Ephesus (*c.* 540–*c.* 480 B.C.) is said to have been a pupil of Xenophanes, but this is doubtful. We have over a

[11] Diels, 21 B 15; Kirk and Raven, No. 172.
[12] For Heraclitus, see Bailey, pp. 18-23; Burnet, pp. 130-68; Kirk and Raven, pp. 182-215.

hundred brief and often cryptic utterances said to be due directly to him, as well as many statements about his teachings. Unfortunately, Zeno (c. 336-264), the founder of the Stoic school, claimed Heraclitus as the author of his own physical doctrines, altering the actual theories to fit Stoic beliefs; and most of our statements about Heraclitus have been more or less influenced by this Stoic adaptation. Thus, Lucretius' criticism of Heraclitus [13] is aimed fully as much at the Stoics of Lucretius' own day as at the philosopher of four centuries earlier.

According to Heraclitus the universe is one of constant, harmonious, balanced change. A flame burning in still air will serve us as an example. In a sense the flame is a continuous thing existing with its own clearly visible properties; but in another sense it is constantly changing, receiving particles from the wick, which become incandescent as they pass up through the flame and vanish as they are consumed at the flame's edge. But to Heraclitus fire is more than an illustration. Fire in the form of the ether that surrounds the world is the ultimate matter, changing into water and then to earth and earthy things, and then back from earth to water and to fire. As far as we know, this process had no beginning and will have no end. If this is so, the belief in the fiery destruction of the world ascribed to Heraclitus by certain ancient writers is certainly a Stoic addition. It is not clear whether this series of changes is rapid and constant, or slow and broken by long seasons of rest. Plato, perhaps with intentional exaggeration, credits Heraclitus with the belief that all things are like the flowing river, which is never the same in two consecutive moments; and this is repeated by Aristotle and those who depended on him for their information. From the actual fragments as distinct from the *testimonia*, we get rather the impression that the process of change from ether to earth and back is slow, and that for any particular object it may be interrupted by long periods of rest. Since this does not violently contradict sensation, and since Heraclitus regarded sensation as the source of knowledge, this last explanation

13 Lucretius, I. 635-704.

may seem most acceptable although it is not the one most often given. One thing at least seems certain. These changes are always in balance—the fire (ether), water, and earth have always been and will always be in the proportions in which they now are. From this it follows that no account of the formation of the world is to be expected from Heraclitus, since according to him it had no beginning.

He seems to have been little interested in astronomy. The sun is a bowl, its open side toward us, filled with fiery exhalations. It is formed anew each morning. Similar explanations are given for other heavenly bodies, but no astronomical mechanism seems to have been provided to account for their motions.

PARMENIDES [14]

Parmenides (fl. *c.* 475 B.C.) of Elea in southern Italy is the last of the monists, the group of philosophers beginning with Thales who sought to explain the world in terms of a single ultimate unity. Those before him had started with the evidence of the senses and had tried to construct theories that explained the manifold variety of the world without too greatly violating what the senses tell us. Parmenides totally disregarded sensation as a source of knowledge, and, starting with the assertion, "What is, is; what is not, is not since it cannot be thought," he carried monism to its logical conclusion—and to its end. The real starting point of his argument is the last part of the statement paraphrased above. Thought, or visualization, is the touchstone of existence. Only that of which we can think can exist. Since we can have no mental picture of "nothing," nothing cannot exist. There is therefore no empty space. What exists, then, can have no empty space within it or outside it, and it therefore cannot move. It cannot have been created since there is nothing other than itself from which it can have been formed; it cannot be destroyed since there is nothing else into which it can pass. Since existence

---

[14] For Parmenides, see Bailey, pp. 24-27; Burnet, pp. 169-96; Kirk and Raven, pp. 263-97.

is all that can be predicated about it, it must be the same in all its parts and extend equally in all directions. That which exists, then, is a solid, undifferentiated, unchanging sphere, uncreated and indestructible, with nothing, not even empty space, about it.

Parmenides, by pushing monism to its logical limit, killed it. A few who followed him supported his theories by ingenious paradoxes aimed chiefly at showing that any other theory was equally contrary to common sense; but there were no new developments in monism after him. The total effect of his teaching, however, was by no means negative. He raised certain questions that had to be considered by all thinkers from his time on. For one thing, he forced serious consideration of the problem that had not been faced before him but has been one of the central problems of philosophy ever since: the nature and source of knowledge. When sensation, reason, and intuition are in conflict, which should be accepted? More important for our present purposes, his uncompromising monism, although at the opposite pole from atomism, actually pointed the way to it. One of his followers, Melissus, trying to prove that the universe must be such a "one" as Parmenides had described, argued, "But if the many exist, they must each be such as the 'one' of Parmenides." When we come to the atomic theories we shall find that this is true. Like the "one" of Parmenides, each atom is solid, unchanging, uncreated, and eternal; but the atoms are infinite in number instead of one, and instead of being at rest, they are in ceaseless motion through an infinite void, the existence of which is as necessary as is that of the atoms themselves. Before the atomists, however, there were others who tried to solve the dilemma created by Parmenides.

EMPEDOCLES [15]

Empedocles of Acragas (fl. *c.* 450 B.C.) agreed with Parmenides that the world was a sphere and was eternal, without

[15] For Empedocles, see Bailey, pp. 27-34; Burnet, pp. 197-250; Kirk and Raven, pp. 320-61.

beginning or end, and that there was no empty space. Parmenides' sphere, however, was composed of a single substance, and he had insisted that out of the one the many could not be formed. Empedocles met this by teaching that the sphere was composed not of one substance but of four—earth, air, fire, and water—and that from the ever-changing combinations of these four all the things of the world that we know are formed. The philosophers before Parmenides had taken motion for granted, but after him this was impossible; and Empedocles introduced two forces, Love and Strife, which cause the motions and the combinations of the four elements. Of these, Love brings unlike things together and separates like things, while Strife does the opposite, bringing together like things and separating the unlike. Since incorporeal existence was still beyond the compass of Greek thinking, Empedocles did not picture Love and Strife as immaterial forces. They are corporeal—really two more elements added to the four named above.

The sphere with its four elements, or rather six, is eternal; but it is constantly passing through a cycle of four changing states. In one state Love is completely victorious and has driven Strife to the outer periphery, while within the sphere Love has brought earth, air, fire, and water into a complete and uniform mixture. In the next state, Strife, forcing its way in from the outer boundary, gradually drives Love out; and at the same time it separates the four elements each after its own kind. The completion of this process marks the third state in which Strife is victorious, the four elements are separated, and Love is on the outside. In the fourth state Love overcomes Strife, and at its end the sphere is as it was at the beginning. This cycle is without beginning or end. Clearly a world such as ours could exist only in the second or fourth of these states; and there is some slight evidence that Empedocles actually placed it in the second.

From the three hundred and fifty scattered lines that remain from his poem *On Nature*, we can see that Empedocles had worked out both sets of changes with a wealth of ingenious detail, but this need not concern us. We can also learn a little

about his astronomy. The earth is surrounded by two hemi-
spheres, one of fire, which causes day, and one of darkness
mixed with a little fire, which causes night and its stars. He
knew that the moon shines by reflected light, and he understood the true cause of eclipses. Strangely, he believed that
the sun also shines by reflected light, presumably the light
from the bright hemisphere reflected from the earth's surface.
Thus the day is caused not by the sun but by the bright hemisphere, and the sun shines only because it is day.

Sensation is explained as the recognition of like by like. The
earth in us responds in some way to earthy parts in other
things, and so with each of the other elements. Sight is due to
effluences from the object seen, which come to the eye and
cause vision. Thought is located in the blood, particularly in
that about the heart, because the blood has equal portions of
all the elements. Consciousness thus seems to depend on the
combination of the elements, which ought to mean that the
soul is mortal. However, in another poem, *The Purifications,*
of which much less survives, Empedocles speaks of reincar-
nation, transmigration, and the final escape of the soul to a
state of bliss. How the two views were reconciled, if they were,
is unknown.

ANAXAGORAS [16]

We probably have more reliable information about the life
of Anaxagoras of Clyzomenae than about that of any of the
other pre-Socratic philosophers, and less real understanding
of his beliefs. He was born about 500 B.C., came to Athens
where he lived for many years before his exile, and died in
Lampsacus at the age of seventy or seventy-five, after having
lived there long enough to gain the regard of its citizens. In
Athens he had been a friend of Pericles, and his prosecution
for "impiety" was quite certainly instigated by enemies of that
statesman, who were not yet strong enough to attack Pericles

[16] For Anaxagoras, see Bailey, pp. 34-45 and 537-58; Burnet, pp. 251-75;
Kirk and Raven, pp. 362-94.

but could lay charges against his friends. It is quite certain that he wrote' only one book, which Socrates in Plato's *Apology* tells us could often be bought for one drachma, a statement that may indicate that the book was brief.

About twenty-three fragments of this book remain, and they defy certain interpretation. The ancient statements about the theories are of interest chiefly in showing that these were often misunderstood in antiquity. To take the example most closely at hand, it is inconceivable that a man of Anaxagoras' stature (and there seems no question among the ancients as to his real importance in the development of thought) could have seriously maintained the views ascribed to him by Lucretius (I. 830-920). If we neglect the *testimonia* and confine ourselves to the actual fragments, the following statements emerge: (1) Matter can be neither created nor destroyed. (2) A thing can be formed only of that which is like itself. (3) Matter is infinitely divisible. (4) Each thing contains portions of all things. (5) Each thing is that of which it contains the most. The first of these statements agrees with the monism of Parmenides, and the second does not contradict it; but the third emphatically denies the Parmenidean idea of the one sole eternal existence, and the last two are developed from the third.

We shall find that the atomists supposed the existence of an infinite number of invisible particles, each of them like the universe of Parmenides, differing from each other in shape and size, but all of the same substance, and not subject to division. The matter of Anaxagoras, on the other hand, is subject to infinite division, and each particle however small still has the qualities that we associate with some one sensible object, yet contains within itself portions of all the sensible objects in the formation of which it may share; that is, each contains portions of all. Anaxagoras, perhaps unconsciously, was applying to physical matter what was proper to geometry. A geometrical line contains an infinite number of points, and this is true no matter how short the line. (He was not troubled by the converse of this: no matter how many points are put together they do not form even the shortest line.) If this is assumed to be true of matter, then, however finely matter is subdivided, each particle will still contain infinite parts and so each may contain portions of all things. Finally, at each stage in the process of division, each particle and each created thing are that of which they contain the most.

Let us see what this would mean in the case of the food that we eat, which becomes bone, blood, flesh, and hair. (The use of mathematical terms is quite foreign to the thinking of Anaxagoras, but it may make the matter clearer to the modern reader.) Suppose that we have four kernels of wheat. Since matter is infinitely divisible, each kernel will consist of an infinite number of parts. We can suppose that 50 per cent of each kernel is made up of a mixture of all things, that 20 per cent of each is wheat, and that the remaining part of each is made up of flesh, blood, bone, and hair in equal proportions. Each kernel thus contains all things, but each is that of which it contains the most, namely wheat. Now these four kernels are eaten and, in the process of digestion, their parts are redistributed into four new units. As before, 50 per cent of each of these consists of all things mixed together and 20 per cent is wheat, but the flesh, blood, bone, and hair are now concentrated, each making up 30 per cent of one of the units. Each unit will now be that of which it contains the most, namely flesh, blood, bone, or hair. These have been formed from the wheat, but nothing has been created or destroyed, and nothing has changed from what it was. What we now recognize after the apparent change was already present before it, and each of the four new units contains portions of all things as did each of the four kernels of wheat. Since matter is infinitely divisible, we could start, not with a kernel of wheat, but with the most minute portion of one, and proceed in the same way. This illustration is, of course, too specific and at the same time too simple; but it may suggest the principle according to which Anaxagoras tried to explain the far more complicated processes of nature.

One essential point has thus far been omitted. We have remarked that after Parmenides it was necessary to give some

cause for motion and change. For Anaxagoras the cause was
Nous, a word ordinarily meaning "mind" but here having a
special meaning and best left untranslated. *Nous* may come a
little closer to being an immaterial power than were the Love
and Strife of Empedocles, but it is still described in physical
terms. It differs from all other things in the universe in that it
always remains pure and unmixed, never containing a portion
of anything else. Before the formation of our world (which
seems to be regarded as one of many, past, present, and future), there was simply a mass of undifferentiated matter,
which had the appearance of air since it contained more of
this than of anything else. *Nous,* being outside this mass, set
a portion of it revolving, and the revolution became greater
and greater, causing the separation of the parts, the earth in
the center with the heavenly bodies revolving about it. Plato
makes Socrates, in the *Phaedo,* complain that after *Nous*
started this revolution it did nothing more—that from this
point all depended on chance. This may be true as far as the
formation of the world is concerned; but we are told that
Nous entered into some things yet not into all. The presence
of *Nous,* which we may here call "mind," quite certainly dis-
tinguishes animate from inanimate things; but beyond this
and a few fragments about the senses we know little of the
psychology of Anaxagoras. Since *Nous* always keeps itself pure
and unmixed, we can safely assume that on the death of a man
his mind returned to the main body of *Nous;* but this is far
from a belief in individual immortality such as Empedocles
seems to have envisaged in his *Purifications.*

LEUCIPPUS AND DEMOCRITUS [17]

   With Leucippus (fl. *c.* 430 B.C.) and his greater pupil, Democritus of Abdera (fl. *c.* 420 B.C.), we finally come to the atomic
theory. Leucippus may have written one book, *The Greater
World System,* although this is also ascribed to Democritus,

   [17] For Leucippus and Democritus, see Bailey, pp. 64-214; Burnet, pp.
330-49; Kirk and Raven, pp. 400-26.

who was one of the most voluminous writers of antiquity. Some seventy works of his, probably most of them short, are listed by Diogenes Laertius,[18] running the whole gamut from *On Harmony* to *On Fighting in Armor*. Twenty-one of these belong to the field of physics in its broad sense, but nearly all of the almost three hundred surviving fragments of Democritus' writings come from his ethical works. For our information on his physical theories, as on those of Leucippus, we have to depend on what was said of them by others, usually in criticism. Ancient writers as a rule group the two together, citing their theories as if they were the result of a joint effort. It is rarely possible for us today to discover any specific points on which Democritus advanced beyond his senior, but it is usually assumed that the theory in its broad outlines was the work of Leucippus, and that it was then elaborated and developed in detail by the younger man.[19]

The atomists start with the law of the permanence of matter, which we have seen was already accepted by some of their predecessors; but for the atomists this matter exists in the form of atoms—indivisible particles, all composed of the same substance, each of them possessing as its sole properties shape, size, mass varying directly with the size, and ceaseless motion. These atoms are indestructible either because they possess no parts (Leucippus) or because they have no void within them (Democritus). They are infinite in number, and they are infinitely varied in their forms. Leucippus believes that they are all so small as to be far below the reach of human senses; but Democritus admits the possibility that if the shapes are of infinite variety, some of the atoms will be large enough to be visible.

In addition to the atoms, there is the void in which they move. Empedocles, although he denied the reality of the void, seems tacitly to have assumed its presence in order to make motion possible. Leucippus and Democritus are the first frankly

---

[18] Diogenes Laertius, *Lives of Eminent Philosophers* IX. 46-49.

[19] Bailey makes an effort to distinguish the contributions of the two, but is not too successful.

to proclaim empty space as an immaterial existence, perhaps not real in the same sense as matter, but certainly as essential. Void makes possible the motion of the atoms; however tightly the atoms may be united, there is always void between them, and therefore there is still the possibility of continued motion by the individual atoms within the complex. With homogeneous matter and no void, only the changeless Parmenidean sphere could exist. Even if exchange between parts within that sphere were possible, nothing would really be changed since all the parts are identical. With void and with the homogeneous matter existing as eternal, ever-moving particles of various shapes and sizes, the infinite variety of the world of sense is possible while the basic substance of all things remains one.

Aristotle complains that neither Leucippus nor Democritus gives any cause for the motion of the atoms. They would probably have replied that the atoms, which have always existed and will always exist, have always been in motion and will always remain in motion, and that their motion no more requires explanation than does their very existence. We may suppose that the original motion of the atoms (if we may speak of "original" when dealing with that which never had an origin) was random, but the actual motion of the atoms is conditioned by their collisions with each other. After colliding, the atoms rebound and may resume their free flight in an altered direction; but sometimes they become entangled with each other and remain close together although each still retains its motion in some fashion, perhaps in the form of vibration. There is some indication that Democritus worked out in considerable detail the relation between the different atomic shapes and the complexes that they might form, probably following the same general principles that we later find in Lucretius.

Leucippus and Democritus gave an account of the origin of our world out of a portion of the infinite number of eternal atoms. These atoms, happening to come together in space and to impart to each other a rotary motion, assumed the form of a great vortex. Since the larger atoms (or more probably the larger complexes of atoms) because of their greater mass offered more resistance to the rotary motion than did the smaller, they gathered in the center as do pebbles or grains of sand in the center of an eddy of water.[20] (This tendency to the center in the vortex, and so in our world, can be identified with weight, which in this earlier form of the atomic system is not a property of the atom but results from its mass and the motion of the whirl.) These larger bodies formed the earth, while the lesser atoms and complexes were thrust out or up, forming the air and the heavenly bodies. Since space and matter are infinite and since the formation of our world was due solely to the atoms moving according to their own laws, the number of other worlds, past, present, and future, like or unlike ours, is also infinite.

The sensations are explained in terms of changes brought about in the soul by external contacts. The soul, composed of spherical atoms and scattered throughout the body, is moved by a touch from without, and it in turn moves the mind, which is composed of similar atoms concentrated in the breast. Touch in the ordinary sense is easiest to explain. It probably was regarded by Democritus as the truest of the sensations, not only because it is the most direct but also because it gives information only about size, shape, mass, and motion, the properties that are present in the atoms and therefore the only properties that are actually possessed by material things in general. In taste we have an actual contact as we do in touch; but a thing's taste is not a real property of the thing tasted, only a special interpretation given by the tongue to the real properties. Taste is therefore subjective, and depends upon the one who does the tasting as well as upon the thing tasted. With smell the subjective element is the same; and since the particles causing smell have to pass through the air from their source to our nostrils, another possibility of uncertainty is introduced.

Hearing and sight are also subjective, since they interpret the real properties of the object in terms of sound and color, which are not real, and they require a more elaborate and less

20 For the cosmic whirl, see note *c* on Epicurus, *Letter to Pythocles* (Appendix, p. 84).

trustworthy mechanism to bring about the contact. Sound is material, a bundle of atoms emitted by the source, passing through the air and striking the ear. Sight is more complicated. Leucippus seems to have been content to borrow from Empedocles the theory of effluences or "idols" given off by the object in unending succession and impinging upon the eye, an explanation that Epicurus later adopted. Democritus, however, combined this with the belief that what is seen is not the object itself nor its idol, but the image that is actually visible in the pupil of the eye. The object and the eye both give off effluences. These meet, and the image of the object is formed in the air and returns into the eye, which then sees it. The chances of distortion are considerable, and although the shape, size, and motion of the objects are real, its color can be only the eyes' interpretation of the real atomic properties. It would appear that Democritus had little trust in the validity of sensation; and since he says that thought and sensation are the same, we might expect his skepticism to be complete. To some extent, the fragments and *testimonia* support this expectation; yet he clearly did believe that the truth about nature, that is, about the atoms and the void, could be known, and that this knowledge depended ultimately upon the evidence of the senses. How he reconciled these two positions is not known. In fact, it is quite possible that he did not recognize their incompatibility or make any effort to reconcile them. Neither do we know what effort, if any, he made to explain the great difficulty in any materialistic system, the step from the physical contact and the physical motion of the soul atoms caused by it to the conscious interpretation of that motion in terms of sensation and thought; or, to state the difficulty in other terms, the difference between the inanimate and the animate, between matter and spirit.

CONCLUSION

With Leucippus and Democritus we have come to the end of the great formative period in the Greek effort to give a rational explanation of the world in purely material terms. Starting with an instinctive feeling that there must be one basic substance in some way underlying the manifold, changing world of sense, the monists had presented their various theories. Thales had seen water as the basis of all existence, but he probably had not gone beyond the bare assertion; Anaximander, with a true feeling that the basic substance must be something different from any of the things of sense, had posited the "undefined"; Anaximenes, taking air as his basic matter, had sought to explain its changes by rarefaction and condensation; Heraclitus had formed all things from fire as it moved along the way up or the way down. All these explanations were open to the criticism that we find several times repeated by Lucretius: "If ever a thing is changed and departs from its proper limits, that is at once the end of that which was before." [21] Next, Parmenides stated the monistic theory in its most absolute and unambiguous form. The basic substance can never submit to change of any sort. It has always been and will always be such as it is now, the same, one and immovable; and aside from it, nothing exists.

There were three answers to this. Empedocles agreed that matter was eternal and that its sum never changed; but for him matter existed in the form of four elements—earth, air, fire, and water—which, alternately combining and separating under the compulsions of Strife and Love, formed our world and, after its passing, will form others in an endless series. This preserved the totality and the eternity of the world; but it substituted four basic elements for one and was still open to the objection that when the elements joined to create some other thing, they ceased to exist and were replaced by the new thing, formed from something different from itself. Anaxagoras, on the other hand, posited a basic matter such that the most infinitesimal particle contained portions of all things and might therefore share in the creation of any of those things

---

[21] Lucretius, I. 670-71, 792-93, II. 753-54, III. 519-20. For a fuller statement, see Epicurus, *Letter to Herodotus* 54.

without changing its nature. He thus hoped to avoid any change in the character of matter as the various things were formed; but in place of a basic unity, multiplicity was carried down to the smallest part. Finally, in the atomism of Leucippus and Democritus, the basic matter is one and the same and is indestructible; but it exists in minute particles of many shapes and sizes, infinite in number, in constant motion through the infinite void, whose existence is now first clearly asserted. These particles have always existed and will always exist, each one unchanging in itself; but by their many constantly changing combinations they make up the changing, multiform world. Matter is still of one sort, but the void makes possible its division and motion, and this in turn makes possible this world and many others, like it or unlike it, through infinite time and space. This theory, ignored by Plato and rejected by Aristotle, was further refined by Epicurus and made the basis of his ethical system. It is best known to us, in the absence of most of the master's works, in the poem *On Nature*, by his Roman disciple, Lucretius.

II. Epicurus

LIFE OF EPICURUS

Our chief source of the life of Epicurus [22] is Diogenes Laertius, whose biography, called "excellent" by DeWitt (p. 6) and by Bailey (*Atomists*, p. 221) a "patchwork," forms the

---

[22] Accounts of the life and teachings of Epicurus will be found in any of the standard works on Greek philosophy. There have been only three books published in English in recent years dealing primarily with him: Cyril Bailey's *Greek Atomists and Epicurus*, referred to in n. *a* above; Bailey's edition of all that remains of Epicurus' writings, with translation and commentary (Oxford, 1926); and N. W. DeWitt's *Epicurus and his Philosophy* (Minneapolis, 1954). Bailey is conventional and sound. DeWitt writes with great fervor, intent on showing that Epicurus was not a mere hedonist (and no competent scholar today believes that he was), and that he placed intuition alongside of sensation as a source of

first part of Book Ten of his *Lives of the Philosophers*.[23] A translation of the more important sections of this appears below (pp. 3-7).

The father of Epicurus, Neocles, was among the colonists sent from Athens to Samos in the middle of the fourth century. Epicurus himself was born about 341 B.C., either in Athens or Samos, and certainly spent his early years on the island. He claimed to have turned to the study of philosophy when he was fourteen. He was about eighteen when Alexander the Great died in 323, and he spent part of the troubled period that followed in Athens, part in various towns of the Asia Minor coast, where he doubtless heard the discussions of the various philosophers of the time and read the works of their predecessors. In 311, at the age of about thirty, he gathered a few disciples about himself, and a few years later moved to Athens. There he purchased the home in which he lived until his death at the age of about seventy and also the "Garden" which formed the site of his school and gave it its name. As far as we can tell, he did not teach in a formal way, but he and his followers lived quietly and without luxury, seeking the happiness that came from the simple life. Many

---

knowledge (which would certainly have surprised Lucretius, who had much better sources than can any scholar of today). Before using DeWitt, a student is advised to read such reviews of his book as those by von Fritz, *Classical Philology*, L (1955), 262-66, or Elder, *American Journal of Philology*, LXXVII (1956), 75-84.

23 Laertius, who wrote in the second century after Christ, seems to have used second- or third-hand material of very uneven value and to have been entirely uncritical in his use of it. In Book X, for example, the three letters and the *Principal Doctrines* quite certainly go back to Epicurus or at least to his immediate successors, and the lists of works seem sound; but much of the biography itself is on the level of gossip. The whole work of Laertius has been edited and translated by R. D. Hicks in the Loeb Classical Library, and the reader is referred to the introduction of Volume One of that edition for a somewhat more favorable estimate of Laertius' method of work and of the value of the *Lives*. The text of all of Laertius is very unsatisfactory, but Book X has benefited from the work of Usener, von der Muehll, Bailey, and Arrighetti. (For details see "Texts and Translations" in the Bibliography, p. xxxix.)

details, true or false, can be found in Laertius, including
Epicurus' last testament with its thoughtful care for the welfare of his friends.

WORKS

Like Democritus, Epicurus was a voluminous writer. Laertius (sections 27-28) has preserved a list of the titles of his
works. *On Nature* in thirty-seven books must have contained
the fullest statement of his physical teachings, which furnish
the foundation for his ethics. Like all the rest of his longer
works, this treatise is lost except for trifling quotations in
other writers and a considerable number of tantalizing scraps
from Herculaneum. These papyrus fragments, which come
from rolls that once formed the library of an Epicurean
scholar, unfortunately give little real information. It is sometimes possible to identify the subject under discussion, but it
is rare that one can be sure what is being said about it. The
Greater Epitome (not in Laertius' list), in which Epicurus
seems to have presented his physical doctrines in somewhat
shorter form, was probably the chief immediate source for
Lucretius. Of Epicurus' total literary output we have, aside
from the short passages quoted by others and the papyrus fragments, only the three *Letters* and the forty *Principal Doctrines*
that Laertius included in his *Life,* and a collection of brief
Sayings found in a manuscript now in the Vatican Library.
These are all translated in the present work.

PHYSICS

In the years between Democritus and Epicurus, there seems
to have been only one change in the atomic theory, and we
do not know to whom it should be ascribed. As we have seen,
the atoms of Democritus had no weight and no tendency to
move downward or to the center until their chance motions
had resulted in the formation of a vortex such as that from
which our world was formed. The original motion seems to
have been random and just as much a part of an atom as were

its shape and mass. Outside a vortex the motion of a particular atom at a given time would be the end result of its original motion and a series of collisions with other atoms. Within a vortex, and so within our world, there would also be a tendency toward the center. Apparently, someone after Democritus made this tendency to the center, now stated as a tendency downward (i.e., weight), the primary cause of atomic motion, and explained the collisions as due to the more rapid fall of the heavier atoms. In any case, Epicurus, followed by Lucretius, assumes that the atoms have weight and that their normal motion is downward; and both are at pains to point out that the velocity of bodies falling through the void would not be affected by their varying weights, and that therefore this unnamed predecessor is wrong in explaining the collisions as caused by varying rates of fall.

The chief innovation in Epicurean physics, the uncaused swerve of the atom, seeks to solve the problem created by this substitution of downward motion in parallel courses at a uniform velocity for the previous random motion of the atoms. The swerve also, as we shall see below, makes possible the freedom of the human will. According to the new physical theory, at indeterminate times and places any of the atoms may swerve and strike other atoms. These in turn are forced from their normal courses, and the series of collisions is thus set up that is necessary for the formation of complexes of atoms and, eventually, of sensible bodies. This swerve has been criticized both in antiquity and today as a wanton violation of the basic principles of the atomists, but it is not altogether contrary to modern physical theory, which recognizes at the atomic level changes to which no cause can be assigned and which seem to follow the laws of probability rather than those of mechanics.

ETHICS

For our knowledge of Epicurus' ethical doctrines we have his own brief statement of theory and practice in the *Letter* to *Menoeceus* (pp. 53-59) and also in certain of the *Doctrines* and *Sayings* (pp. 60-72). However, Lucretius, on whom we lean most heavily for an understanding of the physical theories, gives little connected information about the ethics.[24]

In a purely materialistic system, where thought and will are due to atomic motion and where every atomic motion is caused and controlled by previous motions, freedom of the will is impossible. It is quite probable that Epicurus felt that the chief importance of the atomic swerve lay in the fact that this uncaused motion broke the otherwise unending chain of cause and effect. We do not know how he related the atomic swerve and the freedom of the individual will. In fact, in his extant writings there is no mention of the swerve itself (see *Letter to Herodotus* 43, and note); and the connection between the swerve and the will is made by Lucretius only in a passage (II. 251-93) in which, regarding the freedom of the will as an observed fact that requires no proof, he argues that this freedom proves that the atoms must at some time swerve without a previous cause. That Epicurus placed great weight on man's freedom to choose is, however, clear from section 134 of the *Letter to Menoeceus*, where he writes: "It would be better to accept the myth about the gods than to be a slave to the determinism of the physicists."

＊ It is because man does have freedom of the will that a system of ethics is both possible and necessary. Epicurus developed his ethics directly from his physics. Since the soul is, like all else, a temporary combination of ever-changing atoms, death, which is merely the dissolution of that combination, brings a complete and final end to consciousness. The atoms, of course, continue to exist, but the soul as an individual existence is no more. From this Epicurus reasons that since there can be neither reward nor punishment after death, man's highest good must be sought in this life. He further asserts that

---

[24] There are many passages scattered through the *De Rerum Natura*, e.g., at the beginning of Book II, which show that Lucretius agreed with his master, but there is nothing in the way of a regularly developed and formal treatment of ethics.

happiness is the only thing that is sought for itself and not as a means to something else. Happiness, therefore, is to him the highest good. Just as the sensations are the criteria of knowledge, so the feelings are the criteria of happiness. The wise man, however, will weigh various forms of happiness and will avoid those that involve pain. Indeed, happiness can be defined as freedom from pain, and in particular from the pain caused by unfulfilled desires. The best way therefore to gain happiness is to limit the desires, seeking only those things that are natural and necessary and that bring happiness without pain. The truly wise man is he who can be content, and therefore happy, with a little. It follows from this that in many actual situations the true Epicurean and the Stoic would follow much the same course and make the same choices, although for quite different reasons. Since, however, true Epicureans seem to have been few or at least to have attracted little attention, the teachings of Epicurus soon became an excuse for self-centered hedonism, and the term "Epicurean" on most men's lips came to have the meaning that it usually has today.

III. Lucretius

FROM EPICURUS TO LUCRETIUS

As far as physics is concerned, there seems to have been no progress in Epicurean theory after the master's death. This may have resulted from Epicurus' own attitude, for he claimed that his system was complete and perfect, and that he alone had discovered it, acknowledging no debt to any who had gone before him and holding out no hope for any improvements in the future. At all events, his followers were content to take the physics for granted as the foundation for the ethical system, in which they were more interested, and to make no particular effort to explain, or even to understand, the theories. The Roman poet Lucretius seems to have been the first to set forth the whole physical system anew, and he constantly claims that he is merely presenting the teachings as Epicurus left them. He seems to have worked with one of the lost treatises, probably the *Greater Epitome,* constantly before him; it is therefore reasonably safe to accept the *De Rerum Natura* as the fullest and most accurate statement of Epicurus' original teachings now extant. This explains the constant references to Lucretius in the notes that accompany the present translation. Often, the best commentary on an obscure passage in Epicurus is Lucretius' fuller treatment of the same topic.

THE "DE RERUM NATURA"

Of Lucretius' life, almost nothing is known beyond the fact that he lived in the earlier half of the first century before Christ. He seems to have been a poet of a single poem, the *De Rerum Natura,* a title best translated *On Nature,*[25] which consists of six books averaging a little more than twelve hundred lines in length. In Books One and Two the general principles of the atomic system are set forth. In Book Three, these principles are applied to the human soul, for the mortality of which repeated proofs are given, and the book ends with a triumph song over the fear of death. Book Four deals with sensation and thought, then takes up certain bodily functions, and ends with a bitter attack on the passion of love. In Book Five, we have first an account of the earth and the heavenly bodies, and then a history of the development of human culture. Book Six treats of certain unrelated phenomena of earth and sky, and closes with an account of the plague at Athens.

Lucretius makes his purpose in writing the poem clear from the onset (I. 80-135), and he does not let the reader forget it for any length of time. The poet was profoundly, if wrongly,

---

[25] The standard edition of Lucretius is that by Cyril Bailey (Oxford, 1947). It is in three volumes, the first containing Introduction, Latin text, and English translation, and the other two being filled with an exhaustive commentary. Greek passages in the Introduction and Commentary are usually translated, but a good reading knowledge of Latin is necessary for full use of either. The Liberal Arts Press will soon publish a new translation of Lucretius by the present author, intended as a companion volume to this translation of Epicurus.

convinced that all the evils to which man is heir stem from two things: fear of death and what lies beyond it, and fear of the arbitrary power of the gods. No one can read Plutarch's account of the prodigies that accompanied the assassination of Caesar (largely reproduced in Shakespeare's play), or the portents and their expiation that are seriously recorded in Livy's history for nearly every year from 219 to the end of the extant books without realizing the grip that superstitions had laid on the mind of the ordinary Roman. The old native religion, long perverted by Greek influence and corrupted by politics, could give little comfort, and the newer cults from the East only fanned the flame. Cicero and his group could look with scorn on all this, but Lucretius may have been closer to the heart of the average Roman. The poet believed that if a man could rid himself of such fears, he would be able to live in peace and contentment; he also believed that the one way to secure this release was through an understanding of Nature and her laws, that is, through a knowledge of Epicurean physics.[26] If death is nothing but complete unconsciousness, it is no more to be feared than a dreamless sleep. If all phenomena can be explained by natural law, then the gods need not be feared, although they may still be worshiped as examples of perfect happiness. All this was implicit in Epicureanism from the beginning, but never before had it been so put in the forefront. On the other hand, what had been prominent, the happy life secured by the limitation of desires, is mentioned by Lucretius only in passing.

EPICUREAN PHYSICS AFTER LUCRETIUS

Although the atomic explanation of the universe remained the basis for Epicureanism, it was of little interest to most of the later Epicureans and seems to have been almost forgotten.

26 Farrington, in his stimulating but controversial *Science and Politics in the Ancient World* (London, 1939), argues with great vigor that what Lucretius was attacking was not the superstition of the common man but the state religion manipulated through the machinery of augury by the aristocracy for their own advantage.

Because it was stained with the brush of hedonism, it was thrust into the background by the Christian Church. Interest in it was revived by the French philosopher and scientist, Pierre Gassendi (1592-1655); and the system was restated on the basis of experimental science by Dalton (1766-1844). Gassendi was certainly influenced by his acquaintance with Epicurus and Lucretius, but the atomic system of modern times owes little except this initial impulse to the system of the Greeks. The modern reader, however, if familiar with what are now accepted as facts, will find striking anticipations of some of these in the ancient writers, anticipations based not on evidence from controlled experiment but upon imaginative deduction from uncontrolled observations of the natural world.

BIBLIOGRAPHY

(Limited, except for Greek and Latin texts, to works in English)

TEXTS AND TRANSLATIONS OF EPICURUS

ARRIGHETTI, GRAZIANO. *Epicuro, Opere, Introduzione, testo critico, traduzione e note.* Torino, 1960. This is the most complete collection of Epicurus' works. Although it does not have all the *testimonia* to be found in Usener's edition, it does have many papyrus fragments that had not been deciphered in 1887. The Italian translation faces the Greek text, and there is a brief commentary in Italian at the back of the volume. Unfortunately, this edition appeared after my translation was ready for the press.

BAILEY, CYRIL. *Epicurus, the Extant Remains.* Oxford, 1926. This contains Greek text and English translation of the *Letters,* the *Principal Doctrines,* the remaining portions of Laertius' *Life of Epicurus,* the *Vatican Sayings,* and many fragments, with Introduction and Commentary.

HICKS, R. D. *Diogenes Laertius, Lives of Eminent Philosophers, with an English Translation* ("Loeb Classical Library"). 2 vols. Cambridge, Mass., 1925. Book X, "The Life of Epicurus," containing the *Letters* and the *Principal Doctrines,* is in Vol. II.

VON DER MUEHLL, P. *Epicuri epistulae tres et ratae sententiae e Laertio Diogene servatae; accedit Gnomologium Epicureum vaticanum.* Lipsiae, 1922.

USENER, H. *Epicurea.* Lipsiae, 1887. This contains Laertius' *Life of Epicurus,* including the *Letters* and the *Principal Doctrines,* and a very large collection of fragments and *testimonia.* A German translation of all except the *testimonia* is included.

TEXTS AND TRANSLATIONS OF LUCRETIUS

BAILEY, CYRIL. *Titi Lucreti Cari De Rerum Natura Libri Sex, edited with Prolegomena, Critical Apparatus, Translation, and Commentary.* 3 vols. Oxford, 1947. Quotations from Greek writers are usually translated, but one without a working knowledge of Latin will find difficulty in using the Introduction and the Commentary.

ROUSE, W. H. D. *Lucretius, De Rerum Natura, with an English Translation* ("Loeb Classical Library"). Cambridge, Mass., 1924.

Attention is called to a translation of Lucretius, parallel to the present translation of Epicurus and like it provided with Introduction and Commentary intended primarily for the nonclassical reader, soon to be issued by the Liberal Arts Press Division of the Bobbs-Merrill Company.

TEXTS AND TRANSLATIONS OF THE EARLY GREEK PHILOSOPHERS

DIELS, HERMANN. *Die Fragmente der Vorsokratiker, griechisch und deutsch.* 10th edition by WALTER KRANZ. 3 vols. Berlin, 1961. This is the most complete collection of the fragments of the pre-Socratic philosophers and of statements made about them by ancient writers. The fragments but not the *testimonia* are translated into German.

FREEMAN, KATHLEEN. *Ancilla to the Pre-Socratic Philosophers, a Complete Translation of the Fragments in Diels'* Fragmente der Vorsokratiker. Cambridge, Mass., 1948.

WORKS ON EPICURUS

BAILEY, CYRIL. *The Greek Atomists and Epicurus.* Oxford, 1928.

FARRINGTON, BENJAMIN. *Science and Politics in the Ancient World.* London, 1939.

DeWitt, Norman W. *Epicurus and his Philosophy*. Minneapolis, 1954.

Hicks, R. D. *Stoic and Epicurean*. New York, 1910.

De Lacy, Philip. "Some Recent Publications on Epicurus and Epicureanism (1937-1954)," *Classical Weekly*, XLVIII (1954-55), 169 ff.

WORKS ON EARLY GREEK PHILOSOPHY

Burnet, J. *Early Greek Philosophy*. 4th edition. London, 1930. (A paperbound reprint is available.)

Freeman, Kathleen. *The Pre-Socratic Philosophers, a Companion to Diels'* Fragmente der Vorsokratiker. Cambridge, Mass., 1946.

Kirk, G. S., and Raven, J. E. *The Presocratic Philosophers*. Cambridge, England, 1957. (A paperbound reprint is available.)

Minar, E. L. "A Survey of Recent Work in Pre-Socratic Philosophy (1945-54)," *Classical Weekly*, XLVII (1953-54), 161-70, 177-82.

LETTERS,

PRINCIPAL DOCTRINES,

AND

VATICAN SAYINGS

LIFE OF EPICURUS

Diogenes Laertius' Life of Epicurus begins with a brief account of his birth in Athens in 341 B.C., his education, his contacts with older philosophers, and the beginning of his school (sections 1-3). This is interrupted by some samples of the bitter attacks made upon him (3-8), after which Laertius (or his source) comes to the philosopher's defense (9-12). We are then given another account of his birth, life, and death (12-16), which is followed by his last will and testament given verbatim (16-22). Next come brief statements about some of his followers with lists of their writings (22-26). Thereafter Laertius finally turns to Epicurus' own literary activity, and it is at this point that the present translation begins.[1]

Epicurus was the author of very many books, surpassing all   26b
men in the number of his works. Indeed, they fill nearly three hundred rolls; and in them is contained no statement on the authority of another, but all are the utterances of Epicurus himself. Chrysippus tried to emulate him in the multiplicity of his writings, according to Carneades, who calls Chrysippus the parasite of books and says:

> For if Epicurus wrote something, Chrysippus out of rivalry also produced a work of the same volume. For this reason   27
> he has often repeated himself and has written whatever came into his head, failing to correct errors in his haste; and the passages copied are so many that these alone fill his books. This is also to be found in the works of Zeno and of Aristotle.

Of such extent and value are the works of Epicurus. The most important of them are as follows: *On Nature* (thirty-seven

---

[1] This and all subsequent summaries, printed in italic type, have been added by the translator.

3

books);[2] *On Atoms and Void; On Love; Epitome of the Works Against the Physicists; Against the Megarians; Problems; Principal Doctrines;[3] What to Choose and What to Avoid; On the Chief Good; On the Basis of Judgment,* or *The Canon; Chaeredemus; On Gods; On Piety; Hegesianax; On Lives* (four books); *On Justice in Action; Neocles, to Themista;[4] Symposium; Eurylochus, to Metrodorus; On Sight; On the Angle in the Atom; On Contact;[5] On Destiny; Maxims on Suffering, to Timocrates; Prophecy; Exhortation; On Idols; On Presentation to the Consciousness;[6] Aristoboulus; On Music; On Justice and the Other Virtues; On Gifts and Gratitude; Polymedes; Timocrates* (three books); *Metrodorus* (five books); *Antidorus* (two books); *Maxims on Diseases, to Mithres; Callistolas; On Kingship; Anaximenes; Letters.*[7]

28a

2 Fragments of papyrus rolls that once contained certain books of Epicurus' *On Nature* have been found at Herculaneum. Their condition is such, however, that they add very little to our knowledge of his theories, although they do give some indication of the subjects included in that work. Book II, for example, dealt with sensation, and there are some fairly complete passages on the velocity of the "idols." In Book IX, the phenomena of the cosmos were considered, perhaps chiefly the relation of the earth to the rest of the universe. Book XII treated, *inter alia*, of the shapes of the heavenly bodies and of eclipses. Apparently the discussion of the atoms and the void began in Books XIV and XV. The next fragments are from Book XXVII and seem to deal with methods of argument and proof. Other fragments that cannot be assigned to particular books of the *On Nature* contain references to sensation, memory, and logical thought, to necessity, and to language.

3 The *Principal Doctrines* were included by Laertius at the end of his tenth book, and are translated below (pp. 60-65).

4 Quite certainly we should understand that the work was dedicated to Themista, and similar titles below should be taken in the same way; but the word translated "to" is the same as that which certainly means "against" in the fourth and fifth titles in the list.

5 *On the Angle in the Atom* and *On Contact* probably considered the different shapes of the atoms and the relation of these shapes to the varying sensations.

6 *On Idols* and *On Presentation to the Consciousness* must also have treated sensation and cognition.

7 The general title *Letters* would include the three letters that are preserved by Laertius and are our chief direct source of information in re-

The opinions that Epicurus expressed in these works I shall 28b
try to present by subjoining three of his letters in which he
gives in outline his whole philosophy; and I shall add his 29
Principal Doctrines and any other passages that seem worthy
of quotation so that you will be able to study him from all
sides and reach some judgment upon him. First is the *Letter
to Herodotus,* ⟨which deals with natural science; second, the
Letter to Pythocles,⟩ 8 which deals with the phenomena of
the atmosphere and the heavens; third, the *Letter to Menoeceus,* in which the ethical theory is contained. We shall begin
with the first letter, but before taking that up I shall speak
briefly about the divisions of his philosophy.

His philosophy is divided into three parts, dealing respec- 30
tively with methods of proof, with the natural physical world,
and with ethics. The methods of proof, which are contained
in the work called the *Canon,*9 are the means through which
the other parts are approached. His belief about the physical
world is presented in full in the thirty-seven books *On Nature,*
and in an abridged form in the letters. Ethics deals with
choice and rejection, and is contained in the books *On Lives,*
in the letters, and in the work entitled *On the Chief Good.*
The Epicureans usually treat the methods of proof along with
physics, saying that they deal with the determination of truth
and with the first principle, and that this study is basic. They
say that the subject matter of physics is generation, dissolution, and the natural world; and that ethics deals with things
to be chosen and those to be rejected, with the manner of life,
and with the purposes of living.

They reject theoretical logic on the ground that it draws 31a

---

gard to the teachings of Epicurus. But there seems also to have been a
large collection of his personal letters to friends that was in some way preserved by his school. There are a few quotations from these letters in
ancient writers whose works are extant, and we now have many tantalizing
bits in the papyrus fragments.

8 Supplied by Usener.

9 Literally, "Rule" or "Measure."

the seeker after truth aside from his purpose. It is enough for
the student of the natural world to make progress in accordance with the direct evidence of the phenomena themselves. Thus in the *Canon* Epicurus says that the bases on
which the truth is to be judged are the sensations, the concepts, and the feelings. To these the Epicureans add the
mental apprehension of appearances.[a] He says this himself in
the epitome addressed to Herodotus and in the *Principal
Doctrines.*[10]

Start

31b The individual sensation, he says, does not depend on the
reason and does not admit the recollection of an earlier sensation. It cannot set itself in motion but must be stirred by
something external, and when so stirred it can neither add
anything nor take anything away. There is nothing that can
32 refute a sensation; for the sensation received by one sense cannot refute another of the same sense since both are equally
valid, nor can a sensation received by one sense refute one
received by another, since their subject matter is different.
Reason cannot deny the truth of sensation, for all reason depends upon sensation; nor can one sense contradict another,
for we pay equal attention to all.[11] Also, the fact that our perceptions are in agreement guarantees the reliability of the
senses. Our sight and our hearing are in agreement, as is also
our feeling.[12] Since sensation is valid, we must accept from
things that we can perceive indications about things beyond
the reach of the senses.[13] Indeed, all our ideas are framed
from sensations as we experience and compare them, recognize
their similarities, and combine them, not without the assist-

[a] All superior letters refer to Appendix notes, pp. 75-89.

[10] *Letter to Herodotus* 38b; *Principal Doctrines* XXIV.

[11] See Lucretius, IV. 478-99; Epicurus, *Principal Doctrines* XXIII.

[12] For example, the sight and sound of a flying bee and the pain of
its sting form a harmonious unit that may be repeated, and each of the
sensations guarantees the others.

[13] Either because the latter are too small (like the atoms), too distant
(like the stars), wholly intangible (like the void), or too tenuous (like the
gods).

ance of our reason. Even visions seen by madmen or in dreams are real, for they stir the mind, and that which is not real does not do so.[b ̄]

By "concept" they mean a mental picture, right opinion, notion, or general idea that has been stored up—in other words, the memory of something external that has often been the subject of sensation, as for example the concept that such and such is a man. As soon as you hear the word "man," the image, man, is at once mentally formed in accordance with the concept, which was originally due to sensation. The basic meaning of each word is clear. If we did not first know the thing for which we are searching, we could not search for it; when we say that this which stands before us is a horse or a cow, we must already know by means of a concept the shape of a horse or cow. We could not give a name to anything if we did not already know its form by means of a concept. Therefore, concepts are clear evidence.

33a

Opinion depends upon something previously clearly seen to which we mentally refer when we express the opinion. For example, from what do we know that such and such is a man?[14] They also call opinion a supposition, and they say that it may be true or false: if it is confirmed or not contradicted by evidence, it is true; but if it is not confirmed or is contradicted, it is false. From this was developed the idea of the "problem awaiting solution," as for example the problem of the distant tower that awaits our near approach and the ascertainment of its shape when seen from close by.[c]

33b

34a

There are, they say, two feelings, pleasure and pain, which belong to every living creature, the former being in harmony with its nature, the latter alien to it. By the feelings we decide between acceptance and avoidance. Of investigations, some concern things, some mere words.

34b

This is the summary of Epicurus' views on the divisions of philosophy and on the bases of judgment. We must now turn to the letter.

[14] The opinion expressed depends on the comparison of the thing seen with the clear vision of the mental concept.

LETTER TO HERODOTUS

I. Introduction

A. REASONS FOR THE LETTER

This letter presents a brief compendium of the physics to refresh the memories of those already familiar with the theories.

Epicurus to Herodotus, greeting.

35   Some, Herodotus, are not able to study carefully all my works on natural science or to examine closely the longer treatises. For them I have already written an epitome of the whole system [1] so that they may acquire a fair grasp of at least the general principles and thereby have confidence in themselves on the chief points whenever they take up the study of physics. Those, too, who have acquired a reasonably complete view of all the parts ought to keep in mind an outline of the principles of the whole; for such a comprehensive

36   grasp is often required, the details not so often. You must continually return to these primary principles and memorize them thoroughly enough to secure a grasp of the essential parts of the system. Accurate knowledge of the details will follow if once you have understood and memorized the outline of the whole. Even for the thoroughly trained student this is the most important result of his accurate knowledge: he is able to make immediate use of the things he perceives and of the resulting concepts [2] by assigning them to the simple classes

---

[1] Called the *Greater Epitome*, in contrast to the present letter, to which the name *Lesser Epitome* was sometimes applied (see *Letter to Pythocles* 85a). The *Greater Epitome* was probably Lucretius' chief source. This work does not appear in the list in Laertius.

[2] See note *a* on *Life of Epicurus* (Appendix, p. 76). In the rest of the sentence I translate Usener's text.

and calling them by their own names; for it is not possible for anyone to hold in mind in condensed form the whole interrelated system unless he is able to comprehend by means of short formulas all that might be expressed in detail. There- 37a fore, since such a course is useful to all who are engaged with natural science, I, who recommend continuous activity in this field and am myself gaining peaceful happiness from just this life, have composed for you such a brief compendium of the chief principles of my teaching as a whole.[a]

B. METHODS OF PROOF

Words must be used in their natural meanings. All natural science rests on the evidence of the senses.

First, Herodotus, we must understand the meanings of 37b words in order that by expressing our opinions, investigations, and problems in exact terms, we may reach judgments and not use empty phrases, leaving matters undecided although we argue endlessly. We must accept without further explanation 38a the first mental image brought up by each word if we are to have any standard to which to refer a particular inquiry, problem, or opinion.

Next, we must use our sensations as the foundation of all 38b our investigations; that is, we must base investigations on the mental apprehensions,[3] upon the purposeful use of the several senses that furnish us with knowledge, and upon our imme- diate feelings.[4] In these ways we can form judgments on those matters that can be confirmed by the senses and also on those beyond their reach.[b]

[3] That is, upon the apprehension by the mind of the mental concepts that are themselves the result of repeated sensations (see *Life of Epicurus* 31a; *Principal Doctrines* XXIV; and notes).

[4] The feelings are concerned with ethical matters only.

II. The Universe

A. BASIC PRINCIPLES

Matter can be neither created nor destroyed. The universe as a whole is unchanging.[5]

38c   Now that this has been established we must consider the phenomena that cannot be perceived by the senses. The first principle is that nothing can be created from the non-existent;[6] for otherwise any thing would be formed from any
39a thing without the need of seed. If all that disappears were destroyed into the non-existent, all matter would be destroyed, since that into which it would be dissolved has no existence.[7] Truly this universe has always been such as it now is, and so it shall always be; for there is nothing into which it can change,[c] and there is nothing outside the universe that can enter into it and bring about a change.

B. ATOMS AND THE VOID

The universe consists of matter, recognized by the senses, and void, in which matter moves. Other conceivable things are "accidents" or "properties" of these. Sensible objects are composed of atoms, which themselves are indestructible.[8]

39b   Moreover, the universe consists of material bodies and void.[9] That the bodies exist is made clear to all by sensation itself, on

---

[5] See Lucretius, I. 159-264, II. 62-79, 294-307.

[6] See Democritus, as paraphrased by Diogenes Laertius, IX. 44: "Nothing is formed from the non-existent, and nothing passes into the non-existent" (Diels, 68 A 1).

[7] Before this sentence, we would expect a general statement of the indestructibility of matter, this sentence then furnishing the proof.

[8] See Lucretius, I. 418-502.

[9] After the opening phrase of this sentence, we find in the manuscripts the following: "This he also says in the *Greater Epitome* near the beginning and in Book One of *On Nature*." This is clearly a note added after the time of the author, which has found its way into the text. There are many similar "scholia" in the letters. In this translation they will be ignored unless they add some real information, in which case they will be translated in the notes, with the word "Scholium" preceding.

which reason must base its judgment in regard to what is im-   40a
perceptible, as I have said above. If that which we call "void"
and "space" and "the untouchable" did not exist, the particles
of matter would have no place in which to exist or through
which to move, as it is clear they do move.

In addition to these two, there is nothing that we can grasp   40b
in the mind, either through concepts or through analogy with
concepts,[10] that has real existence and is not referred to merely
as a property or an accident of material things or of the void.

Of material things, some are compounds, others are the   40c
simple particles from which the compounds are formed. The   41a
particles are indivisible [11] and unchangeable, as is necessary
if all is not to be dissolved to nothing, but something strong
is to remain after the dissolution of the compounds, something
solid, which cannot be destroyed in any way. Therefore, it is
necessary that the first beginnings be indivisible particles of
matter.

C. THE INFINITY OF THE UNIVERSE

i. *The universe is infinite, for there is nothing to bound
it, and each of its elements is also infinite.*[12]

Moreover, the universe as a whole is infinite, for whatever   41b
is limited has an outermost edge to limit it, and such an edge
is defined by something beyond.*d* Since the universe does not
have an edge, it has no limit; and since it lacks a limit, it is
infinite and unbounded. Moreover, the universe is infinite
both in the number of its atoms and in the extent of its void.
If, on the one hand, the void were infinite and matter finite,   42a
the atoms would not remain anywhere but would be carried
away and scattered through the infinite void, since there
would be no atoms from without to support them and hold

10 That is, either through mental images formed by emanations received by the senses or directly by the mind from material things, or
through mental combinations of these images.

11 The Greek word is *atoma,* properly an adjective meaning "that
cannot be cut."

12 See Lucretius, I. 958-1051.

them together by striking them. If, on the other hand, the void were finite, there would not be room in it for an infinite number of atoms.

> ii. *To account for the differences in sensible objects, the atoms must exist in many forms, the number of different forms being inconceivably great but not infinite, while the number of atoms of each form is infinite.*[13]

42b   In addition, the indivisible, solid particles of matter, from which composite bodies are formed and into which such bodies are dissolved, exist in so many different shapes that the mind cannot grasp their number; for it would not be possible for visible objects to exhibit such great variation in form and quality if they were made by repeated use of atoms of conceivable variety. The number of atoms of each shape is infinite; but the number of varieties cannot be infinite, only inconceivably great.[14]

D. THE MOTION OF THE ATOMS

> *The atoms move continuously, both freely in space, and with more limited motion forming gases, liquids, and solids. This motion had no beginning.*[15]

43   The atoms move without interruption through all time.[16] Some of them ⟨fall in a straight line; some swerve from their courses; and others move back and forth as the result of collisions. These last make up the objects that our senses recognize. Some of those that move in this way after collisions⟩ [17] separate far from each other; the others maintain a

[13] See secs. 55b-56a below, and Lucretius, II. 333-580.

[14] Scholium: "Nor can division, as he says below, continue without end. And he says, since the qualities change, if one is not going to increase the atoms in size without limit [?]."

[15] The motion of the atoms is also discussed in secs. 60-62 below. Some disarrangement of the text seems probable. See Lucretius, II. 62-332.

[16] Scholium: "And he says below that they also move with the same velocity since the void yields equally to the lightest and the heaviest."

[17] Most editors suppose a lacuna at about this point; and some such supplement as that given is needed to make the statement here agree with that of Lucretius, II. 216-93.

vibrating motion, either closely entangled with each other or
confined by other atoms that have become entangled.*^e^ There   44
are two reasons for this continued vibration. The nature of
the void that separates each of the atoms from the next permits it, for the void is not able to offer any resistance; and
the elasticity *^f^ that is characteristic of the atoms causes them
to rebound after each collision. The degree of entanglement of
the atoms determines the extent of the recoil from the collision. These motions had no beginning, for the atoms and the
void have always existed.[18]

If all these things are remembered, a statement as brief as   45a
this provides a sufficient outline for our understanding of the
nature of that which exists.

E. THE INFINITE NUMBER OF WORLDS

*Because atoms and space are infinite, the number of worlds,
like or unlike ours, is also infinite.*[19]

Finally, the number of worlds, some like ours and some   45b
unlike, is also infinite. For the atoms are infinite in number,
as has been shown above, and they move through the greatest
distances. The atoms suited for the creation and maintenance
of a world have not been used up in the formation of a single
world or of a limited number of them, whether like our world
or different from it. There is nothing therefore that will stand
in the way of there being an infinite number of worlds.

[18] Scholium: "He says below that the atoms have no qualities except
shape, size, and mass. He says in the *Twelve Rudiments* that color changes
with the position of the atoms. The atoms are not of all sizes; certainly
no atom is perceived by the senses." The paragraph which now follows
in the text would be more appropriate if it came after the brief section,
"The Infinite Number of Worlds," which now has the appearance of
being an afterthought.

[19] See Lucretius, II. 1048-76.

III. Sense Perception

A. SIGHT

i. *Thin films, which we call "idols," are constantly given off by objects, retaining the form and color of the object.*[20]

46a   Moreover, there are images of the same shape as the solid bodies from which they come but in thinness far surpassing anything that the senses can perceive. It is not impossible *g* that emanations of this sort are formed in the air that surrounds a body, that there are opportunities for the creation of these thin, hollow films, and that the particles composing them retain as they flow from the solid object the same position and relative order [21] that they had while on its surface. Such images we call "idols." [22]

ii. *Because their unsurpassed fineness frees them from internal and external collisions, the idols move with almost atomic speed.*[23]

47b   Nothing in nature as we see it prevents our believing that the idols are of a texture unsurpassed in fineness. For this reason, their velocity is also unsurpassed, since they always find a proper passage, and since moreover their course is retarded by few if any collisions, while a body made up of an inconceivably large number of atoms [24] suffers many collisions as soon as it begins to move.*h*

---

20 See Lucretius, IV. 54-129.

21 By keeping the same position (orientation), they retain the color of the object (see scholium, n. 18 above); by keeping the same relative order, its shape.

22 What appears in the text of Diogenes Laertius as the last part of sec. 46 seems to belong at the end of sec. 61; and the first part of sec. 47 seems to belong at the end of sec. 62. They are so placed in this translation, with the numbers 46b and 47a.

23 See Lucretius, IV. 143-215.

24 As is any perceptible body.

iii. *These films, which are replaced by new matter as soon as they leave the surfaces of bodies, usually retain their forms; but sometimes a new idol is formed in midair.*

Moreover, there is nothing to prevent our believing that the creation of idols is as swift as thought. They flow from the surfaces of a body in a constant stream, but this is not made evident by any decrease in the size of the body since other atoms are flooding in. For a long time the idols keep their atoms in the same relative position and order that they occupied on the surface of the solid, although sometimes the idols do become confused, and sometimes they combine in the air.[25] This combination takes place quickly since there is no need of filling up their substance within. There are also some other ways in which idols come into being. No one of these statements is contradicted by sensation if we examine the ways in which sensation brings us clear visions of external objects and of the relations between them.

iv. *Both thought and sight are due to idols coming from objects to us.*

We must suppose that we see or think of the outer form of a thing when something comes to us from its surface. We could not as readily perceive the color and shape of external objects by means of impressions made on the air that lies between us and them, or by means of rays or beams of some sort sent from us to them,[26] as we can when outlines of some kind, like the objects in color and shape and of the proper size to affect either our eyes or our minds, come to us from the objects. Since these move in rapid succession they present a single uninterrupted image; and they maintain a quality in harmony with their source because their energy, which has been im-

48

49

50a

[25] This may mean either that a new idol may be formed from atoms in midair, or that two existing idols may combine and form a compound idol. According to Epicurean theory, both of these are possible. See Lucretius, IV. 129-42, 722-44.

[26] See the theory of Democritus, Introduction, pp. xxvi-xxvii.

parted to them by the vibrations of the atoms in the depths of
the solid object, is itself proportionate to the energy of that
source.[i]

v. *The mental picture from the intent look or the concentrated thought is true. Error results when opinion adds
something.*[27]

50b   When, by the purposeful use of our mind or of our organs
or sense, we receive a mental picture of the shape of an object or of its concomitant qualities, this picture is true, since
it is created by the continuous impact of the idols or by an
impression left by one of them.[j] Whatever is false and erroneous is due to what opinion adds ⟨to an image that is waiting⟩
to be confirmed, or at least not to be contradicted, by further
evidence of the senses, and which then fails to be so confirmed
51   ⟨or is contradicted⟩.[28] The mental pictures that we receive in
the images that either come to our minds in sleep or are
formed by the purposeful use of the mind or of the other
instruments of judgment would not have such similarity to
those things that exist and that we call true if there were
not some such material effluence actually coming to us from
the objects; and the errors would not occur if we did not permit in ourselves some other activity similar ⟨to the purposeful
apprehension of mental images⟩ but yet different. From this
other activity [29] error results if its conclusions are not confirmed by further evidence or are contradicted, but truth if
52a   they are so confirmed or are not contradicted. Therefore, we
must do our best to hold opinion in check [30] in order that we
may neither destroy the criteria of judgment, which depend on
the clear view, nor confuse everything by placing erroneous
opinion on an equality with firmly established truth.

27 See Lucretius, IV. 462-68; Epicurus, *Principal Doctrines* XXIV.

28 Scholium: "in accordance with some motion in ourselves, which is
not unlike mental visualization, but is faulty and is the cause of error."

29 That is, from the additions of opinion to the mental image. The
three supplements in this paragraph are by Usener.

30 Or: "to maintain this principle."

B. HEARING

An effluence from the source of sound, splitting up into
particles each like the whole, which come in sequence to
the ear, causes hearing.[31]

Moreover, we hear when a kind of stream is carried to our   52b
ears from a person who speaks or from an object that makes
a sound or noise or in any way whatever arouses in us the
sense of hearing. This stream divides into particles, each of
which is of the same nature as the whole, and these particles
preserve a common relationship to each other and a peculiar
continuity that extends back to the source of the sound and
usually arouses comprehension in the hearer; or if it fails to
do this, it at least makes clear that there is something outside.
Without some common relationship extending out from the   53a
source, there would not be such awareness. We must not suppose that the air itself receives an impression from the spoken
word or sound,[32] for indeed the air is far from admitting any
such thing. Rather, the force that is created in us when we
speak causes such a displacement of particles, capable of
forming a breathlike stream, that it produces in the person to
whom we are speaking the sensation of hearing.

C. SMELL

Effluences likewise rouse the sense of smell.[33]

We must also suppose that, like sounds, smells could not   53b
produce any sensation if there were not carried from the object certain particles of a nature proper to stir the organ of
this sense. Some of these are disorderly and unpleasant; some
are gentle and agreeable.

[31] See Lucretius, IV. 524-614.
[32] The theory of Democritus (Bailey, *Atomists*, pp. 170-72; Kirk and
Raven, p. 423).
[33] See Lucretius, IV. 673-86.

IV. The Atoms

A. PROPERTIES OF THE ATOMS

i. *The unchanging atoms possess no qualities save size, mass, and shape. Other qualities result from atomic position or motion.*[34]

54   We must suppose that the atoms possess none of the qualities of visible things except shape, mass, and size, and whatever is a necessary concomitant of shape.[35] For every quality changes; but the atoms do not change in any way, since in the dissolution of composite things something hard and indestructible must survive that will make changes possible—not changes into nothingness and from nothingness, but changes brought about by alterations in the positions of some atoms and by the addition or removal of some. It is necessary that the particles that alter their positions and come and go be indestructible, not sharing in the nature of the visible things that are changed, but having their own peculiar shapes and

55a   masses; for this much must be unalterable. Even among sensible things, we see that those that are altered by the loss of matter on all sides still retain shape; but the other qualities do not survive in the changing object, as shape survives, but are removed from the whole body.[k] These properties that remain are enough to cause the differences in composite things, since it is necessary that something survive and be not utterly destroyed.

ii. *The atoms vary in size, but are not of every size, for if they were, some would be visible.*[36]

55b   We must not think that there are atoms of every size lest the visible world prove us wrong; yet we must suppose that

---

[34] See Lucretius, II. 730-864.

[35] For example, roughness or smoothness.

[36] At II. 499, Lucretius speaks of the small size of the atoms as something he has already proved; but the passage containing the proof, if it was ever written, has been lost.

there are some differences in size. If there are some differences, it will be easier to explain our feelings and sensations. But the atoms need not be of every size in order to account for the differences in qualities; and if they were of every size, some would necessarily be large enough for us to see.[37] It is clear that this is not the case, and it is impossible to think how an atom might become visible. 56a

B. THE PARTS OF THE ATOM

i. *We cannot assume matter to be infinitely divisible. A thing containing infinite material parts, no matter how small they were, would itself be infinitely large.*[38]

Next, we cannot suppose that in a finite body the parts, no matter how small, are infinite in number. Therefore, not only must we exclude infinite division into smaller and smaller parts lest we make everything weak,[l] and in our conception of the parts that compose a whole be compelled to make them less and less, finally reducing real things to nothingness; but also in dealing with finite things we must not accept as possible an infinite progression to parts each smaller than the last.[m] For if once you say that in a finite thing there are parts infinite in number even if of the least possible size, you cannot think how this can be. For how can a thing containing infinite parts be finite in size? It is clear that the infinite parts are each of some size, and however small they may be, the whole must be infinite in magnitude. 56b 57a

ii. *As in a visible thing there is a smallest part recognizable by the eye, which cannot be seen by itself and the total number of these smallest parts measures the whole, so in the atom there is also a least part recognizable by the mind, which cannot exist by itself, and the total number of these parts measures the atom.*[39]

[37] Both Leucippus and Democritus believed that the atoms were of infinite variety, and Democritus thought that some of them might be visible. See Kirk and Raven, pp. 408-9, n. 2.

[38] See Lucretius, I. 551-98, 615-26.

[39] See Lucretius, I. 599-634.

57b   Again, if in the finite body there is a part that can just
be distinguished by the eye even if it is not visible by itself,
we must believe that there is an adjacent part similar to
this, and that if one went on in this way in his mind from
one point to the next, he could not continue without end.

58   We must suppose that the smallest perceptible part is not like
those bodies that are large enough that we can move our eyes
from one part to another, nor yet is it wholly unlike such
bodies. Although it has some similarity to them,[40] it does not
admit division into parts. But if because of this similarity we
think to mark off mentally a separate portion of the part on
this side or that, we find that we are looking at the similar
part adjacent to it. If, starting out from the first of these parts
and not dwelling on the same one, we inspect them one after
another, we find that they do not touch each other part
against part,[41] but by their own one special characteristic they
measure magnitude, there being many of them in large bodies,
few in small.[42] We must suppose that the least part of the
atom has the same relation to the whole as the least percep-

59   tible part has to the whole visible object. It is clear that the
least part of the atom is smaller than the least perceptible
part, but it has the same relationship to the whole of which it
is a part. We have already stated from its relationship to
sensible bodies that the atom has size, although far inferior
to them in this respect. Furthermore, the uncompounded least
parts of the atoms must be regarded as fixed units, which offer
themselves to us in our mental survey of the invisible as a

40 That is, it is like them in that it has extension, which a geometrical
point lacks.

41 A peculiar but logical idea. Ordinarily, when two bodies are in
contact the left part of one, let us say, touches the right part of the
other. But these smallest visible parts are so small that they themselves
have no visible parts. They therefore appear to us to touch each other,
not part against part, but whole against whole.

42 Their special characteristic is that they have extension but lack
parts. They are therefore suitable units of measurement, since every
visible body will consist of a whole number of such parts with no frac-
tions remaining.

means for the measurement of the atoms, both greater and smaller.[43] The similarity between the least parts of atoms and the least perceptible parts of sensible things [n] is sufficient to justify our reasoning up to this point; but it is not possible that the least parts of atoms ever moved individually and came together.

C. THE MOTION OF THE ATOMS

i. *Although there can be neither top nor bottom in infinite space, the terms up and down have meaning with respect to ourselves.*

Next, we cannot predicate up or down of infinite space as   60
if there were a highest or lowest. Yet if it were possible to draw a line from the point where we are standing upward to infinity in the space above our heads, neither this line nor one drawn downward from the observer to infinity would appear to be at the same time both up and down with reference to the same spot, for this would be nonsense. Thus it is possible to think of one motion extending to infinity in the direction that we call up and one extending down, even if what moves from us into the spaces above our heads comes a thousand times to the feet of those above us and what moves downward comes to the heads of those below; for one of the motions is nonetheless regarded as extending as a whole to infinity in one direction, and the other motion in the other direction.[o]

ii. *The atoms, always moving in the void, always possess equal velocity, whether their motion be caused by collision or by weight. If unchecked, an atom will cross any conceivable distance in an inconceivably short time.[44]*

Moreover, it is necessary that the atoms possess equal ve-   61
locity whenever they are moving through the void and noth-

[43] As each sensible body must consist of a given number of the least visible parts, so each atom must consist of a given whole number of these atomic least parts.

[44] See Lucretius, II. 80-164.

ing collides with them. For heavy bodies will not be carried more quickly than small, light ones when nothing at all opposes them, nor do the small bodies, because they all find suitable passages, excel the large ones, provided the latter are not obstructed.[45] This is equally true of the atoms' motions upwards or to the side because of collisions and of their downward motion because of their own weight.[p] The atom will traverse space with the speed of thought as long as the motion caused in either of these ways maintains itself; that is, until the atom is deflected either by some external force,[46] or by its own weight which counteracts the force of the earlier collision. Moreover, since the motion through the void takes place without any interference from colliding particles, any conceivable distance is completed in an inconceivably brief time. For it is the occurrence or nonoccurrence of collisions that gives the appearance of slow or rapid motion.[q]

46b

> iii. *At any point of time the atoms of a compound body are moving in all directions with atomic speed, but because of their constant collisions and changes of direction, the motion of the body as a whole in any appreciable time may be brought within the reach of our senses.*[47]

62   Although all atoms have the same velocity, it will be said that in the case of compounds some atoms move faster than others. Men will say this because even in the shortest continuous period of time the compound and the atoms in it do move in one direction. However, in points of time recognized only by the reason, the atoms are not in motion in one direction but are constantly colliding with each other until the motion as a continuous whole comes within the reach of our senses.[r] For what opinion adds about what the senses

---

[45] Although the rest of this paragraph deals with the motion of the atoms, this one sentence makes a statement about bodies in general as evidence for the motion of the invisible atoms. It is not so stated, but the reference must be to falling bodies.

[46] By some new collision.

[47] See Lucretius, II. 112-41, 308-32.

cannot perceive, namely that in times perceptible only by the reason there will be a continuity of motion, is not true in the case of the atoms. What is grasped by the purposeful use of the senses or by the mental apprehension of concepts contains the whole truth.[48] We must not suppose that in times   47a
perceptible by the reason the whole moving compound moves in various directions, for this is unthinkable; and if this were true, when the body arrived in a perceptible time from any quarter whatever, the direction from which we observe its motion would not be that from which it originally started. The visible motion of the body will be the result of the internal collisions, even if below the visible level we leave the velocity of the atoms unaffected by the collisions.[g] An understanding of this principle will be useful.

V. The Soul

A. COMPOSITION OF THE SOUL

The soul is material, composed of finely divided particles, some like breath, some like fire, and some of a third, unnamed kind.[49]

Next, referring to the sensations and the feelings as the   63a
most certain foundation for belief, we must see that, in general terms, the soul is a finely divided, material thing, scattered through the whole aggregation of atoms that make up the body,[t] most similar to breath with a certain admixture of heat,[50] in some ways resembling the one, in some ways the other. But there is also a part of the soul that goes beyond even these two in fineness,[u] and for this reason it is more ready to share in the feelings of the boay. All this is made evident to us by the powers of the soul, that is, by its feelings, its rapidity of action, its rational faculties, and its possession of those things whose loss brings death to us.[51]

48 See Diogenes Laertius, *Life of Epicurus* 31a, and notes.
49 See Lucretius, III. 94-322.
50 We must remember that to Epicurus heat was a material substance.
51 See the long discussion in Lucretius, III. 417-829.

B. THE SOUL AND THE BODY IN SENSATION

The soul experiences sensation only when enclosed in the body; and the body receives from the soul a share in this sensation. Sensation may survive the loss of parts of the body, but it ceases with the destruction of the soul or of the whole body.[52]

63b
64   Next, we must conclude that the primary cause of sensation is in the soul; yet it would not have acquired sensation if it had not been in some way enclosed by the rest of the body. But the rest of the body, having given the soul the proper setting for experiencing sensation, has itself also gained from the soul a certain share in this capacity. Yet it does not fully share with the soul, and for this reason when the soul departs, the body no longer experiences sensation; for the body did not have this capacity in itself but made sensation possible for that other that had come into existence along with it, namely the soul. The soul, thanks to the power perfected in it by the motions of the body, at once bringing to completion its own power to experience sensation, returned a share of this power to the body because of their close contact and com-

65   mon feelings, as I have said. For this reason, sensation is never lost while the soul remains, even though other parts of the body have been destroyed. Indeed, even if a portion of the soul is lost with the loss in whole or in part of that portion of the body that enclosed it, if any part at all of the soul survives, it will still experience sensation; but when the rest of the body survives both as a whole and part by part, it has no sensation if that collection of atoms, small though it be, that makes up the soul has been lost. However, if the whole body is destroyed, the soul is scattered and no longer enjoys the same powers and motions; and as a result, it no longer

66   possesses sensation. Whenever that in which the soul has existed is no longer able to confine and hold it in, we cannot

52 See Lucretius, III. 119-23, 323-58, 396-416.

think of the soul as still enjoying sensation, since it would no longer be within its proper system and would no longer have the use of the appropriate motions.[53]

C. MATERIAL NATURE OF THE SOUL

The term "incorporeal" is properly applied only to the void, which cannot act or be acted on. Since the soul can act and be acted upon, it is not incorporeal.[54]

Moreover, we must clearly observe this also, that the word "incorporeal" in its common use is applied only to that which we can think of as existing by itself.[55] Now there is no incorporeal thing that we can think of as existing by itself except the void. The void can neither act nor be acted upon; [56] it only gives to corporeal things a space through which to move. Therefore, those who say that the soul is incorporeal are talking nonsense; for in that case the soul would be unable to act or be acted upon, and we clearly see that the soul is capable of both.

67

D. CONCLUSION

If you refer all this discussion about the soul to your feelings and sensations, remembering what was said at the beginning of the discussion, you will find enough embraced in this outline to enable you, starting from it, to work out the details with certainty.

68a

53 Scholium: "Elsewhere he says: 'The soul is composed of the finest and roundest atoms, much surpassing those of fire. Part of it lacks reasoning power and is distributed through the whole body. The reason is in the breast, as is clear from our fears and joys. Sleep occurs when the parts of the soul that are scattered through the whole organism are held fast or carried apart, then collide because of the impacts. The semen comes from the whole body.' "

54 See Lucretius, III. 161-67.

55 That is, we do not apply the term to attributes or properties (see secs. 68b-71).

56 See Lucretius, I. 454.

VI. Properties and Accidents

A. PROPERTIES

Shape, mass, etc., are properties of things. They cannot exist by themselves; they are not separable parts of the things to which they belong; without them the things could not be perceived.[57]

68b   In the next place, shapes, colors, sizes, mass, and all other things that are spoken of as belonging to a body must be thought of as properties either of bodies in general or of bodies that are perceptible and are recognized by our perception of these properties.[58] These properties are not to be regarded as having existence by themselves, for we cannot think

69   of them apart from things of which they are properties; nor are they wholly without existence. They are not some kind of immaterial thing attached to the body, nor are they parts of the body; but from all of them together the body as a whole receives its permanent character. We do not mean that these properties come together and form the body as happens when a large body is formed from its separate parts, either from the primary parts or from large parts that are smaller than the whole, whatever it is; we merely mean, as I have said, that the whole body receives its own permanent character from the presence in it of these properties. Each of the properties of a body has its own appropriate way of being perceived and distinguished; and the body as a whole is perceived along with its properties, not separately from them, and is identified by this composite recognition.

B. ACCIDENTS

i. *Like properties, accidents can be recognized only in connection with bodies; but they are not permanent attributes as are the properties.*[59]

[57] See Lucretius, I. 449-54.
[58] Shape, size, and mass are properties of all bodies; color, of visible bodies only.
[59] See Lucretius, I. 455-58.

It also often happens that there are qualities that do not   70
permanently accompany bodies. ⟨They, too, do not exist by
themselves, yet they are not wholly without being.⟩ [60] They
do not belong to the class that is below the level of perception, nor are they incorporeal. In applying to them the term
"accidents" in its commonest meaning, we make it clear that
they have neither the nature of the whole that we comprehend as a composite and call "body," nor the nature of the
permanent properties without which a body cannot be
thought of. By the appropriate senses each of them can be
recognized in company with the composite body to which it
belongs; but we see a particular accident only when it is pres-   71
ent with the body, since accidents are not unchanging attend-
ants. We must not deny the reality of this clear vision of the
accidents on the ground that they neither possess the nature
of the whole which they accompany and which we call body,
nor share in its permanent properties; and we must not think
that they exist by themselves, since this is not conceivable for
the accidents or for the properties. They must all be accepted
as what they appear to be, namely accidents belonging to
bodies, not permanent properties nor things having any place
by themselves in nature; but they are seen to have just the
character that our senses ascribe to them.

ii. *Time presents a special problem. We cannot visualize
it, and we can recognize it only as an accident of an event,
which is itself an accident.*[61]

Before turning from this subject, we must carefully con-   72
sider one more matter. Time is not to be sought for like other
things that we seek in an underlying object by comparing
them with the mental images that we look for in our own
minds,[62] but we must consider the clear data of experience by
virtue of which we distinguish between a long time and a

---

[60] A lacuna is recognized here by most editors; some such supplement
as that given seems called for.

[61] See Lucretius, I. 459-82.

[62] One can visualize an object or even a property or an accident in
connection with an object, but one cannot visualize time.

short one, regarding the empirical data as closely allied to
the concept of time. We need not search for better descrip-
tions of time, but we must use the very ones that are at
hand; nor need we assert that something else is of the same
nature as this unique entity, as some indeed do; but we should
take into consideration as of chief importance only the things
with which we associate time and the ways in which we
73a measure it. This requires no elaborate demonstration, only a
review of the facts. We associate time with days and nights
and their parts, and in the same way with changes in our
own feelings and with motion and rest, recognizing that the
very thing that we call time is in its turn a special sort of
accident of these accidents.[63]

VII. The Worlds

A. THE CREATION OF WORLDS

*Each world was formed by being separated from its own
whirling mass, and will be dissolved again.*[64]

73b In addition to what we have said, it is necessary to believe
that the worlds [65] and every limited complex that has a continuous similarity to the visible world have been formed from
the infinite, each of them, greater and smaller, separating out
from its own whirling mass. We must suppose also that these
will all be dissolved again, some more quickly and some more
slowly, some afflicted by one calamity and others by another.[66]
74a One must not suppose that because of necessity worlds in

[63] See Sextus Empiricus, *Against the Mathematicians* X. 219: "Epicurus . . . said that time was an accident of accidents, accompanying days,
nights, seasons, feelings and lack of feeling, motions, and rest" (Usener,
No. 294).

[64] See Lucretius, V. 416-508.

[65] Each world consists of an earth and the heavenly bodies associated
with it. We were told in sec. 45b that the number of worlds is infinite.

[66] Scholium: "It is thus clear that he says that the worlds are subject to
destruction by the changing of their parts. And elsewhere he says that
the earth rests upon air" (see Lucretius, V. 534-48).

a single pattern [67] ⟨were created, or in every possible pattern. . . .

B. FORMS OF LIFE IN THE WORLDS

We may assume animal and vegetable life in the other worlds similar to that on ours.

. . . Moreover, we may believe that in all the worlds there   74b
are animals, plants, and the other things we see;⟩ [68] for no
one can show that the seeds from which grow animals, plants,
and the other things we see might or might not have been included in one particular world and that in another kind of
world this was impossible.[v]

VIII. The Development of Civilization

A. THE ARTS AND CRAFTS

Instinct led men to the first developments, which reason then improved upon.[69]

Moreover, we may assume that by the conditions that sur-   75a
round them, men were taught or forced by instinct to do
many things of many kinds, but reason later elaborated on
what had been begun by instinct and introduced new inven-
tions. In some fields, great progress was made, in others, less;
and in some times and ages reason ⟨had more success in free-
ing men from their fears⟩ of the powers above than in others.[70]

[67] Scholium: "In Book XII of his work *On Nature* he says that these
differ: some are spherical, some are egg-shaped, and the rest are of various shapes; yet they do not have every shape. We must not suppose them
living things separated from the infinite."

[68] A considerable lacuna at the end of the preceding section and the
beginning of this was probably caused by the intrusion of the scholium.
I have translated Usener's supplement. Following this sentence in the
text is the scholium: "So too we may suppose that they would be provided with food in the same way as on the earth."

[69] See the elaborate treatment of the development of culture in
Lucretius, V. 925-1457.

[70] The text of the last part of this sentence is quite uncertain. I have
translated Bignone's text.

B. LANGUAGE

Language was a natural development, differing in different tribes. Later, speech was clarified by deliberate selection.[71]

75b So too we may suppose that in the beginning words did not receive meaning by design. The natural characters of men who underwent different experiences and received different impressions according to their tribes, caused them to emit air from their lips formed in harmony with each of the experiences and impressions, the men of each tribe differing in their own separate ways as the tribes differed because of their dif-

76a fering environments. But later in each race, by common agreement, men assigned particular meanings to particular sounds so that what they said to each other might be less ambiguous and the meaning be more quickly made clear. When men who had known them introduced certain things not previously seen,[72] they assigned names to them, sometimes being forced instinctively to utter the word, but sometimes making their meaning clear by logically selecting the sound in accordance with the general usage.[73]

IX. The Phenomena of the Heavens

A. CAUSES OF CELESTIAL PHENOMENA

No divinity directs the heavenly bodies, for this is inconsistent with divine happiness; nor are they themselves divine.[74]

76b Now as to celestial phenomena, we must believe that these motions, periods, eclipses, risings, settings, and the like do not take place because there is some divinity in charge of them, who so arranges them in order and will maintain them in

---

71 See Lucretius, V. 1028-90, which treats only of the first stage, omitting the part played by convention and reason in the development of language. See also Diodorus of Sicily, I. 8. 3-4.

72 Or possibly: "certain intangible things."

73 That is, by giving a name suggested by the similarity of the new thing to something that had already been named.

74 See Lucretius, V. 110-234, and Epicurus, *Letter to Pythocles, passim.*

that order, and who at the same time enjoys both perfect happiness and immortality; for activity and anxiety, anger and kindness are not in harmony with blessedness, but are found along with weakness, fear, and dependence on one's neighbors. We must also avoid the belief that masses of concentrated fire have attained a state of divine blessedness and undertaken these motions of their own free will. In all the terms with which we set forth our conceptions of such blessedness, we must preserve due reverence lest from irreverent words there grow opinions that deny this majesty. If we fail, this contradiction will cause the greatest confusion in our souls. Therefore we must believe that, at the time of the first formation of these bodies at the creation of the world, the law of their motions was fully ordained.

B. PURPOSES OF, AND LIMITATIONS ON, THE STUDY OF CELESTIAL PHENOMENA

i. *While knowledge of the general principles governing these matters is essential to our happiness, the study of the details is vain. We must accept the possibility of multiple causes.*[75]

Now we must accept the following beliefs: that to acquire exact knowledge about basic causes is the task of natural philosophy; that, as far as the heavenly bodies are concerned, our happiness depends on this basic knowledge and upon knowing the general nature of the visible phenomena of the heavens and whatever is necessary for certainty up to this point; that in these first principles there is neither multiformity nor any possibility of variation; and that in the immortal and blessed nature there is absolutely nothing that causes doubt and confusion. That these statements are true without qualification we can ascertain by reason. But we must also know that whatever belongs to the investigations of settings and risings, periods and eclipses, and the like—that this is of no import for the happiness that comes from knowl-

[75] These theses are implicit throughout Lucretius' fifth book, but are nowhere concisely stated.

edge; and that those who have learned these things but are
ignorant of the original nature and the basic causes are subject to fears as great as if they knew nothing, or perhaps to
even greater fears because the amazement that follows the
study of these phenomena is not able to solve the problem of
their relation to the essential principles.[76] Therefore, if we
find that there are many possible causes for periods, settings,
risings, eclipses, and the like, just as we found many possible
80   causes in our investigation of details,[77] we need not think that
our investigation of these matters has not reached a certainty
sufficient to secure for us peace of mind and happiness. We
must search for the causes of celestial phenomena and in general of that which cannot be clearly perceived by first finding
in how many ways similar phenomena are produced within
the range of our senses; and we must pay no heed to those
who, in the case of phenomena that can only be seen from
a distance, fail to distinguish between that which is and remains single and that which may happen in many different
ways,[78] and who do not know under what conditions it is possible and under what conditions impossible to achieve peace
of mind. If we know this, that phenomena may take place
in many ways, we shall be as little disturbed if we merely
think it possible that a particular phenomenon happens in
some particular way as we would be if we knew this as an
absolute fact.[10]

     ii. *Men imagine that the celestial bodies are divine yet
ascribe to them purposes inconsistent with divinity; and
they anticipate eternal suffering after death. Peace of mind*

[76] Epicurus has in mind astrology and its effect upon its devotees.

[77] For example, in the explanation of eclipses, *Letter to Pythocles*
96b (see Lucretius, V. 751-70). This letter and Book V of Lucretius offer
many other examples.

[78] That is, between the basic principle (the atomic system), which is
fixed and unalterable, and such observed phenomena as eclipses, which
may be caused in different ways at different times and in different worlds.
In the last part of this sentence and in the next, von der Muehll's text
has been followed.

follows freedom from such fears, and will be gained if we trust to our immediate feelings and sensations.[79]

In addition to these general matters, we must observe this also, that there are three things that account for the major disturbances in men's minds. First, they assume that the celestial bodies are blessed and eternal yet have impulses, actions, and purposes quite inconsistent with divinity. Next, they anticipate and foresee eternal suffering as depicted in the myths, or even fear the very lack of consciousness that comes with death as if this could be of concern to them. Finally, they suffer all this, not as a result of reasonable conjecture, but through some sort of unreasoning imagination; and since in imagination they set no limit to suffering, they are beset by turmoil as great as if there were a reasonable basis for their dread, or even greater.[80] But it is peace of mind to have been freed from all this and to have constantly in memory the essential principles of the whole system of belief. We must therefore turn our minds to immediate feelings and sensations [81]—in matters of general concern to the common feelings and sensations of mankind, in personal matters, to our own—and to every immediate evidence from each of the means of judgment.[82] If we heed these, we shall rightly track down the sources of disturbance and fear, and when we have learned the causes of celestial phenomena and of the other occasional happenings, we shall be free from what other men most dread.

81

82a

79 See Lucretius, III. 31-93, V. 55-90.

80 Or, accepting Usener's conjecture, *eikaiōs doxazonti,* for the *ei kai edoxazon* of the manuscripts: "turmoil as great as that which comes to the man who has thought only casually on this matter, or even greater turmoil."

81 Our sensations lead to knowledge of what a thing is; our feelings, chiefly in terms of pleasure and pain, tell us what to seek and what to avoid, that is, what is good and what is evil.

82 See Laertius, *Life of Epicurus* 31a, and note.

X. Conclusion

This summary will be useful both for the beginner and also, as an easily remembered outline, for the more proficient.

82b Here then, Herodotus, you have the most important points in regard to natural science set down in such condensed form 83 that this discourse may be accurately held in mind. I think that one who masters this, even if he does not progress to all the parts of a detailed study, will have very great strength compared with other men. He will also be able of himself to make clear many detailed points in regard to our system as a whole, and these general principles themselves will constantly aid him if he but hold them in memory. For these points are such that those who have made considerable progress and even those who are proficient in the detailed study, by solving their problems with reference to this survey, will make the greatest advances in the knowledge of the whole; and some of those who have made less progress toward perfect knowledge can, hastily and without oral instruction, run through the matters of most importance for peace of mind.[83]

[83] In Laertius, *Life of Epicurus,* this letter is followed by the *Letter to Pythocles,* the following brief paragraph connecting the two letters: "This is his letter on physics; the letter on celestial phenomena follows."

LETTER TO PYTHOCLES

I. Introduction

A. THE OCCASION OF THE LETTER [1]

This brief account of the phenomena of the atmosphere and the heavens is sent as requested.

Epicurus to Pythocles, greeting.   84

Cleon delivered to me a letter from you displaying a kindly feeling toward me worthy of my affection for you, in which you try not without effect to recall the arguments leading to a happy life. In this letter you beg me to send you an account of the things above the earth,[2] short and concise so that you may remember it easily; for what is written in my other books, although as you say you constantly have them in your hands, is difficult to remember. I received your request with pleasure and am filled with agreeable expectations. Now that I have   85a finished all my other writing, I shall carry out what you ask, especially since this explanation will be useful to others also, in particular to those who have only recently tasted the true

[1] It is generally accepted that this letter is not the work of Epicurus himself, but a condensation of parts of several of his works made not long after his death by some follower who contented himself · .th extracting brief passages without connecting them or giving much in the way of explanation or illustration. Thus the *Letter,* although not the work of Epicurus, does preserve his theories and perhaps in many places his very words, and it is, except for Books V and VI of Lucretius, our best evidence for the least satisfactory part of his natural philosophy, namely his treatment of the phenomena of the air and the sky (see Usener, *Epicurea,* pp. xxxvii-xli, and Bailey, *Epicurus,* pp. 275-76).

The Pythocles to whom the letter is addressed was a youthful and beautiful follower of Epicurus. The Cleon of the opening sentence is unknown.

[2] *Ta meteŏra,* a recognized field of knowledge, included the study not only of astronomy but also of atmospheric phenomena such as lightning, whirlwinds, and hail.

teachings about the natural world and to those too deeply
plunged into any of the everyday affairs that leave little
leisure. Receive this then gladly, and read it attentively and
quickly along with what else we sent you in the *Lesser Epitome* addressed to Herodotus.

B. THE PURPOSE OF STUDYING IN THIS FIELD

*The only purpose of studying these phenomena is to secure
peace of mind. Do not expect to find single causes in this
area. We must accept as possible every plausible explanation that is not contradicted by evidence.*[3]

85b   First, do not think that knowledge about the things above
the earth, whether treated as part of a philosophical system
or by itself, has any purpose other than peace of mind and
86   confidence. This is also true of the other studies. Do not at-
tempt the impossible and do not expect to conduct investigations in all fields in the way in which we have discussed
ethics or found solutions for other physical problems (for
instance, the composition of the universe from matter and
void, or the indivisibility of the first elements) or of all problems that have single explanations in agreement with the
visible evidence. For the case is different with the things above
the earth. Each of these phenomena has more than one cause
for its creation and more than one account of its nature, all
of them in harmony with the evidence of the senses. We must
not build up an explanation of Nature according to empty
87   assumptions and dictates, but as phenomena invite; for our
life does not have need for illogical and empty opinions, but
for an existence free from disturbance. If one is satisfied,
as he should be, with that which is shown to be probable, no
difficulty arises in connection with those things that admit of
more than one explanation in harmony with the evidence of
the senses; but if one accepts one explanation and rejects another that is equally in agreement with the evidence, it is
clear that he is altogether rejecting science and taking refuge
in myth. Some of the phenomena that we can observe give

---

[3] See *Letter to Herodotus* 78-82a.

indications about events above us, since they (but not those above) are seen just as they happen; for it is possible that the latter take place in many ways. We must hold fast to the 88a actual appearance of each celestial phenomenon; and in regard to the speculations that we base upon the actual appearance, we must single out those events whose occurrence from one cause or another is not disproved by terrestrial experience.

II. The Worlds

A. DEFINITION AND DESCRIPTION

A world includes an earth and the heavenly bodies about it. It may be of any shape.

A world is a certain limited portion of the universe, en- 88b compassing celestial bodies and earth and all the phenomena, at whose destruction all in it will be thrown into chaos. It is separated from the boundless,[4] and is limited by a boundary either airy [5] or thick, which is either in circular motion or at rest, and either spherical or three-cornered [a] or of any other shape whatever. All variations are possible, for none of the observations of the senses in our world contradict this, since we cannot even perceive the boundaries of this world.

B. CREATION AND DURATION OF WORLDS

The number of worlds is infinite. A world may be created by the accumulation of matter from other worlds or from space. A world endures as long as it receives new matter.[6]

It is possible to assume that such worlds are infinite in 89 number, and that such a world can come into being in either a world or an inter-world (as we call the spaces between

---

[4] See Leucippus: "Worlds are formed in this way: many particles of every shape are cut off from the infinite and are carried into a great empty space" (Diogenes Laertius, IX. 31; Diels, 67 A 1). The text of this paragraph is very uncertain.

[5] According to Lucretius, the boundary of our world is fire or air. See, for example, I. 73: "the flaming walls of our world."

[6] See Lucretius, II. 1048-1174, V. 416-508, 534-63.

worlds),[7] in a place for the most part empty (but not in a great and absolutely empty void as some say),[8] when seeds of the proper kind flow together from one world or inter-world or from many. These gradually get together and join, and they move from place to place, if it so happens; and matter appropriate in nature flows in until the new world is complete and durable, a condition that lasts as long as the foundation underlying it is able to receive new matter.

90a   It is not merely requisite that in the void in which a world is to be formed there be an accumulation of matter or a whirl caused by necessity, as some fancy; and a world cannot increase in size until it strikes another world, as one of the so-called physicists says. For this is contrary to the evidence of phenomena.[b]

C. THE CELESTIAL BODIES

i. *The sun, moon, and stars grew as matter like wind or fire separated out from the whirling mass.*[9]

90b   Sun, moon, and the other celestial bodies were not first formed by themselves and later drawn in by the world, but were formed along with it from the very first and slowly increased as some sort of finely divided matter, like wind or fire or both, was separated out from the whirling mass; for the evidence of our senses suggests this.[c]

ii. *The size of the celestial bodies is about what our senses indicate.*[10]

91   The size of the sun and moon and the other celestial bodies is, for us, such as it seems to be.[11] In reality, it is a little greater than we see it or a little less or about the same; for

[7] Epicurus placed the homes of the gods in the inter-worlds.

[8] See the quotation from Leucippus in n. 4 above.

[9] See Lucretius, V. 432-94.

[10] See Lucretius, V. 564-91.

[11] Scholium: "In Book XI of the work *On Nature* he says: "For if the size has been reduced by distance, the color will be even more reduced. But there is no distance more suitable for causing such reduction." See Lucretius, V. 566-69.

thus our senses record earthly fires when they are seen from
a distance.^d Every objection to this will be easily dissolved if
you are intent on the clear view, as I show in the work *On
Nature.*

iii. *Their motions may be explained in many ways.*^e

Risings and settings of the sun, the moon, and the other   92
celestial bodies may be due to the kindling and quenching of
their fires,[12] the composition of the matter about them at the
points where they rise and set being such as to bring this
about, for nothing in the evidence of the senses contradicts
this. The risings and settings of these bodies may also be
caused by their appearance above the rim of the earth and in
turn by their being covered; for this too is not contrary to the
evidence of the senses. It is not impossible that their motions take place in accord with the revolution of the whole
heaven,[13] or the latter may be fixed, and necessity from the beginning of the world may have decreed the motion of these
bodies toward their rising. . . .[14]

. . . by heat according to some distribution of fire always   93
going on to places in succession. It is possible that the sun
and moon vary their tracks with the seasons because of the
slant forced upon the heavens at these times. But there are
other equally possible causes. There may be a wind blowing
across their lines of motion; or the appropriate fuel may con-

[12] So Heraclitus (Diels, 22 B 6; Kirk and Raven, No. 228).

[13] Not the stars, but whatever part of the world is beyond all the
heavenly bodies that we can see.

[14] As translated, this sentence like those before it refers to the daily
motion of all the heavenly bodies. Bailey takes the words here translated
"toward their rising" as meaning "toward the east," in which case the
motion described must be the apparent delay in the motion of the sun,
moon, and planets relative to the motion of the stars. But this seems
highly improbable, since we are still discussing the motions of all the
celestial bodies, including the stars.

The application of the words following the lacuna is unknown, but
they seem to refer to the theory that the heavenly bodies are really fires
following a line of fuel (see next note).

stantly be set on fire in one place as it burns out in another; [15]
or from the beginning a rotary motion may have been assumed by these heavenly bodies of such a kind that they move
in a sort of spiral. For all such explanations and others akin
to them do not differ from any of the clearly observed phenomena if one, in such fields of inquiry, is able to hold fast
to what is possible and to refer each problem to what agrees
with the evidence of the senses, disregarding the illiberal art
of the empirical astronomers. [16]

   iv. *The phases of the moon may be brought about in var-*
   ious ways. It may shine with its own or with reflected light.
   The face in the moon may be due to differences in its
   surface or to interposition. [17]

94   The alternating waning and waxing of the moon may result
from a rotation of the moon itself, or from the configuration
of the air, or even from the interposition of a body; or they
may be brought about in any of the ways that earthly phenomena suggest to us as explanations of what is seen in the
moon. But we must not, out of desire to have a single explanation, refuse without reason to consider the others, ignoring
the limits of human observation and for this reason seeking
to know that which is impossible. Next, it is possible that the
moon has its own light, but it is also possible that its light
95a is from the sun; for in our experience many things are observed to have their own light from themselves, many from
outside sources. There is nothing in celestial phenomena to
prevent our accepting all of these theories as possible if we
always keep in mind the principle of multiplicity as we ex-

   [15] In this case the sun, for example, is not a body but a fire racing
along a fuse-like line of fuel. This explanation would be more in place
in the first part of the section than here. Possibly a general statement
of this theory has been lost in the lacuna and the present sentence gives
the reason why the sun follows a new course each day.
   [16] These astronomers, by compiling tables of past phenomena (phases
of the moon, eclipses, etc.) may be able to foretell the phenomena to
come, but they have no understanding of the basic principles or causes.
   [17] See Lucretius, V. 575-76, 705-50.

amine the explanations and causes that are consistent with
the evidence and do not turn aside to inconsistent explanations and, giving them weight without reason, slip back,
sometimes in one way, sometimes in another, to the principle
of a single cause.

The appearance of the face on the moon may be the result   95b
of a variation in parts of the moon's surface, or of something
between us and the moon, or of any causes that we observe
in harmony with the evidence of the senses. In investigating   96a
all celestial phenomena, we must not abandon this method;
for if anyone goes contrary to clearly observed facts, he will
never be able to share true peace of mind.

v. *Eclipses of sun and moon may result from the extinction
of their lights or the interposition of other bodies. We must
not assign these matters to the gods.*[18]

The eclipses of the sun and of the moon may be due to   96b
their extinction, as we see lights on earth put out. They may
also result from the interposition of other bodies, either the
earth or some other body that is similar to it but invisible.[19]
In our examination, we must pair causes in harmony with
each other, and we must remember that two simultaneous
causes are not impossible.[20]

Then the regularity of celestial motions must be accounted   97
for just as is that of certain terrestrial events. The gods must
not be drawn into the discussion in any way, but must be left

[18] See Lucretius, V. 751-70.

[19] The text of this sentence is doubtful. Another reading would be
translated " . . . either the earth, ⟨or the moon,⟩ or some invisible body, or
some other similar thing." In the following sentence, we are warned that
we may not, for example, say that the moon shines with its own light,
and then explain its eclipse by its entry into the earth's shadow; or say
that the face on the moon is due to variations in its surface, and then
explain the moon's phases by its rotary motion.

[20] Scholium: "In Book XII of the work *On Nature* he says the same,
and in addition that the sun is eclipsed when the moon throws a shadow,
and the moon, by the shadow of the earth. But eclipses may also be
caused by withdrawals. This is also stated by Diogenes the Epicurean
in Book I of his *Epilecta*."

free from duties and in perfect blessedness. If this warning is neglected, all our explanations of celestial phenomena will be wasted, just as has been true for some who have not held to the method of the possible but have been carried away to what is vain; that is, to the belief that each phenomenon has a single cause. Casting aside all the other possible causes, they are swept into an area where reason does not apply and are unable to take into account the things that are seen, from which we ought to receive suggestions about other things.

vi. *The changing lengths of the days are due to the varying time spent by the sun in his journeys.*[21]

98a   The varying lengths of day and night may be due to the sun's moving over the earth now quickly, now slowly, either because of the changing length of his journey or because he crosses certain places with greater or less speed, as is seen to be the case with some things on earth in accordance with which we must give our explanations about things above. But those who insist on a single cause oppose the evidence of the senses and have wandered far from the way in which a man may learn.[22]

vii. *Weather signs from on high may be due to chance, or there may be a real connection.*

98b   Weather signs [23] may be due to mere coincidence, as is the case with signs from animals about us, or they may be due to actual alterations and changes in the air, for both are in har-
99a   mony with phenomena; but we cannot tell under what conditions a sign is due to this cause or to that.

21 See Lucretius, V. 680-704.
22 In this paragraph I have followed Hicks's text.
23 Apparently signs from celestial bodies, perhaps the stars of the zodiac, which mark the seasons. Weather signs from animals are discussed in sec. 115 below.

III. Phenomena of Our Atmosphere

A. CLOUDS AND RAIN

Clouds may be formed by compression of air or by the gathering of moisture. Rain occurs when clouds are compressed or there is a down draft of air.[24]

Clouds can be formed and take their places both when air [25] is compacted by winds blowing toward each other, and when there is an interlacing of atoms of a sort that cling together and are appropriate to produce this result; and again when currents [26] flow together from the land and the waters. And there are many other ways in which it is not impossible that the formation of clouds takes place.

99b

Rain can be produced from clouds if they are squeezed together, or if some change takes place in them, or again, by a wind blowing through moist air from a suitable quarter. A more severe rain occurs when there is an accumulation of matter suitable to cause such a downpour.

99c
100a

B. THUNDER AND LIGHTNING

i. *Thunder may be caused by wind within clouds, by the rending or friction of clouds, or in other ways.*[27]

The cause of thunder may be air whirling within hollow clouds as within our jars, or the booming within them of fire fanned by air, or the bursting and rending of clouds, or the friction and fracturing of clouds that have congealed into ice crystals. The evidence of our senses requires that we say that thunder, like other things, is produced in many ways.

100b

[24] See Lucretius, VI. 451-526.

[25] The lower air (*aēr*, which is moist, in contrast with the dry upper air, *aithēr*) if pressed together forms clouds. So below, a wind blowing down through this moist air may cause rain.

[26] That is, currents of air that have picked up moisture from the land and sea.

[27] See Lucretius, VI. 96-159.

ii. *Lightning may be caused when the proper atoms are forced from clouds, when fire from the stars falls from clouds where it has gathered, when fiery atoms set clouds on fire, when winds or clouds under strain burst into flame, or in other ways.*[28]

101   The causes of lightning also are many. It may be produced when a mass of atoms, in the proper configuration to cause fire, escapes from clouds that rub against each other or collide, or when atoms of a kind that causes this flash are driven from the clouds by the winds, or when such atoms are squeezed from clouds that are under pressure from each other or from the winds. Or lightning may occur when fire, which has been scattered from the celestial bodies, has been gathered together by the motion of the clouds and the winds and then falls through the clouds; or when fire composed of the finest atoms has penetrated the clouds and the clouds have thereby been set on fire, with thunder resulting from the fire's motion. Again, the cause of lightning may be the igniting of the winds brought about either by the strain of their motion or by ex-
102a   cessive compression; or it may be the bursting of the clouds by the winds and the expulsion of atoms proper for producing fire and for assuming the form of lightning. And it is not diffi- cult for us to see other ways in which lightning may be brought about if we hold fast to the evidence of the senses and are able to compare lightning with earthly phenomena similar to it.

iii. *Lightning precedes thunder because it causes thunder.*[29]

102b   Lightning precedes thunder in such a cloud formation either because the mass of atoms that is to form the lightning is driven out of the cloud at the same time that the blast of wind enters it, and then this wind, pent up in the cloud, makes the noise of thunder; or because both lightning and thunder burst from the cloud at the same time, but the former makes a quicker journey to us while the latter moves more

[28] See Lucretius, VI. 160-63, 173-218.
[29] See Lucretius, VI. 164-72.

slowly, just as is true when we see persons at a distance strik-   103a
ing blows.

iv. *Thunderbolts are produced when fire in the clouds is
unable to penetrate them and a part of it breaks through
and strikes down.*[30]

A thunderbolt *f* may be formed when, after many eddies   103b
of wind are crowded together and have burst violently into
flame, a part of the fire breaks out and falls with even greater
violence on the places below. The reason the break occurs is
that, as the clouds are being compressed, the regions through
which the fires move become successively more and more
tightly packed.*g* A thunderbolt may also be formed by the very
outbreak of the whirling fire (in the same way as thunder is
produced), when the fire, becoming too fierce and being
driven too violently by the wind, is unable to move into the
adjacent regions because of the constantly increasing pressure
of the clouds upon each other, and so bursts its cloud. And   104a
thunderbolts may be produced in many other ways. Only you
must avoid superstition, which you will do if, keeping well
on the track marked by the senses, you gain from them indications about the unseen.

C. CYCLONIC STORMS

*Cyclonic storms occur when a cloud is rotated by the winds,
when a cloud enters a whirling wind, or when winds are
confined by thick air.*[31]

A cyclonic storm may be formed by the column-like descent   104b
of a cloud, which has been forced down to the places beneath
it by a closely packed wind from which it receives a rotary
motion,[32] while at the same time an external wind is driving
it to one side. Such a storm may also be produced from a formation of wind in a circle with a sort of mist driven in from
above, or from a great rush of winds that are not able to move

30 See Lucretius, VI. 219-422.
31 See Lucretius, VI. 423-50.
32 Reading *kuklōi* with Usener.

105a to the side because of the density of the surrounding air. When cyclonic storms, produced from the motion of the wind in any of these ways, are let down over the land, a tornado results; but when over the sea, they cause a waterspout.

IV. Terrestrial Phenomena

A. EARTHQUAKES

Earthquakes are produced by wind shut up in the earth, or by falling masses within the earth.[33]

105b Earthquakes may be produced when wind is shut up in the earth, divided alongside of small masses of earth, and continuously shaken, causing the earth to quiver. Either this wind enters the earth from outside, or air contained in the earth is set in motion within by masses of earth falling into cave-like places. Again, it is possible that earthquakes are produced by the shock wave caused by the fall of many such masses and by the return wave when the first one rebounds from more compact regions of the earth. And there are many other possible 106a causes for these shakings of the earth.

⟨B. VOLCANOES

A volcano is hollow, full of heated air in violent motion, which finally escapes through the mountain's jaws.⟩ These winds are aroused when water or other foreign matter forces its way in.[34]

106b . . . The [35] winds occur from time to time when some foreign substance continually and gradually makes its way in, and

[33] See Lucretius, VI. 535-607.

[34] See Lucretius, VI. 639-702.

[35] There is clearly a lacuna here. The last sentence of the preceding paragraph closes the discussion of earthquakes; and what we have here does not seem to be a part of a general theory of winds. Because of the similarity between this passage and Lucretius, VI. 694-700, Bailey suggests that we have here the conclusion of Epicurus' explanation of volcanic action. The first part of the summary is based on Lucretius, VI. 680-93.

when water collects in large amounts. The remaining winds arise when a few fall into the many hollows, a spreading of these taking place.

V. More Atmospheric Phenomena

A. HAIL

Hail is formed by the freezing and separation of particles like air or like water.

Hail is formed by violent freezing as certain wind-like par-   106c
ticles gather from all sides and are then divided, and also by less violent freezing and simultaneous division of certain water-like particles, their gathering taking place at the same time as their division so that they are formed both as separate units frozen solid and also in groups.[36] It is not impossible   107a
that their shape is spherical because their corners on all sides have melted away, and it may be that when they were formed the individual particles, whether like air or like water, were distributed evenly from all sides, as it is said.

B. SNOW

Mist falling from clouds may freeze and form snow, or snow may be formed in the clouds themselves.

Snow may be produced when from time to time winds   107b
violently compress suitable clouds of proper porousness, and water in the form of mist is forced out. This mist is frozen as it falls by the cold that surrounds it in the region below the clouds. Or such a fall of snow might result from the freezing of moist clouds of uniform density if they lay side by side and rubbed against each other. If these clouds are subject to a sort of pressure they produce hail, which usually happens in the spring.[k] And when clouds that have been frozen are rubbed   108a
together, the accumulated snow takes flight.[l] In other ways, too, snow can be produced.

[36] Both the text and the meaning are very uncertain.

C. DEW, FROST, AND ICE

*Dew is formed when particles of moisture unite on high
and fall. If the air is cold, frost may be formed instead. Ice
is formed when rough particles expel the smoother particles from water.*

108b   Dew is produced when particles suitable for forming moisture of this kind come together from the air; and again, when
particles like this are carried from regions that are damp or
contain bodies of water, places where dew is most often found,
then meet in the air, form water, and finally drop back to the
ground below. Similar things that happen in some such way
109a   ⟨are often seen. Frost⟩ is produced when the drops of dew
⟨undergo change⟩,[37] some of them being in some way frozen
by the presence of cold air. Ice is produced when the round
particles are squeezed out of water and the jagged and angular particles that are present in water are forced together;
and also when such rough particles come into water from outside, are drawn together, and cause the water to solidify, a
portion of the round particles being driven out.

D. THE RAINBOW

The rainbow is caused by sun shining on mist.[38]

109b   A rainbow may result from the sun shining on misty air;
perhaps light and air form a peculiar combination that produces the colors of the rainbow, either all together or separately, and when the light shining on the different parts is
reflected, the air about assumes such color as we see according
110a   to the light that shines on the several parts. The rainbow appears round in shape because all its parts are seen at an equal
distance from our eyes; or else because either the atoms in the
air or those in the mist that are reflected from this same air

37 The supplements, which form a continuous passage in the Greek,
are by Bailey. Usener's somewhat different suggestions would give essentially the same meaning.

38 See Lucretius, VI. 524-26. Both the text and the meaning of the last
sentence of this paragraph are very doubtful.

have taken this shape and therefore what is formed jointly presents this appearance.

VI. More Celestial Phenomena

A. THE HALO AROUND THE MOON

The moon's halo is formed when air moving toward the moon either blocks the moon's rays or solidifies a ring of air.

A halo around the moon is formed when air, carried from all sides toward the moon, either checks the currents of light that flow evenly from the moon to just the point that they form this misty ring and are not scattered in all directions, or compresses the misty air that is about the moon equally on all sides in such a way as to make it circular and thick. This happens in certain parts of the sky when some current of air blows forcefully from outside, or when the heat closes openings in such a way as to bring this about.

110b

111a

B. COMETS

Comets move where fuel is available, or they are disclosed to us by a movement of the sky, or they come into our world from without.

Comets exist when, at certain times and in certain parts of the sky where conditions are right, a fire finds fuel; [39] or when at certain times the heavens above us have some special motion so that these bodies become visible. It is also possible that at certain times the comets themselves begin to move because of special circumstances and, arriving in the regions above us, become visible. They disappear for reasons opposite to these.

111b

C. FIXED STARS AND PLANETS

i. *The stars about the pole never leave the sky.*

Certain stars "revolve in their place." [40] This happens, ac-

112a

[39] See n. 15 above.

[40] An Homeric expression, here used of the stars that revolve about the pole star and never leave their celestial abode by crossing the horizon.

cording to some, because that part of the sky is fixed while
the rest revolves about it; or it may be that an eddy of air
stands about that region in a ring, preventing them from
moving in the same way as do the rest. Finally, it is possible
that the proper fuel for these stars is not found everywhere
but only in the region in which we see them confined. And
you will find many other ways in which this can be accomplished if you can consider what is in agreement with the evidence of the senses.

ii. *Stars and planets may have different motions, either
because this was decreed at the beginning, or for other reasons.*[41]

112b   Some of the stars wander, if it so chance that they really do
follow such courses, but others move in unchanging paths.
113   This may be because stars, moving with circular motions from
the beginning, have been subject to such necessity that some
of them are carried along in the same uniform orbits but
others in orbits that show irregularity. It is also possible that
in some of the regions through which the stars are carried
there are uniform expanses of air that entice the stars constantly in the same course and supply fuel uniformly, and
other levels are so unequal that in them the stars perform the
erratic motions that we see. But to give a single cause for these
things when the evidence of the senses suggests many is mad-
ness and is done foolishly by those who are eager followers of
vain astrology and who pointlessly proclaim the causes of
things while failing to free the divine nature from all burdens.

iii. *The apparent differences in the velocity of the celestial
bodies may be caused in three different ways.*[42]

114a   Some celestial bodies are seen lagging behind others because,
although completing the same revolution, they are carried
through it more slowly; or because, while they are swept along
by the general rotary motion, they have a natural impulse in
the opposite sense; or again, because some are carried through

41 See secs. 92-93 above, and notes.
42 See secs. 92-93 above, and notes; also Lucretius, V. 614-49.

a greater orbit, some through a lesser, although all complete the same cycle.*j* But to give a simple explanation of these things is the act of one who wishes to perform wonders for the crowd.

iv. Falling stars may be bits of stars that have rubbed against each other, or they may be collections of fire atoms.

The stars that are said to fall may be in part caused by the rubbing together of the stars themselves, or by the expulsion of fragments where a blast of wind breaks out, just as we said above about lightning; [43] and they may be formed when there chances to be a meeting of fire-forming atoms in such accord that they do burst into flame and then move on in a direction determined by the forces with which they first met; and finally, a meteor may result when wind gathers in some misty stronghold, is set on fire by the pressure, bursts out from what held it, and hurtles along in whatever direction it may be impelled. And there are other causes untinged by superstition by which this phenomenon can be induced.

114b

115a

VII. Weather Signs from Animals

The weather signs given by animals depend on coincidence.[44] Certainly, the animals cannot compel the winter to end, nor does some divine being watch for these beasts to venture forth and then bring to pass what they have foretold. For such foolishness would not occur to any creature, however humble, if it but had the least wit, far less to a being possessing perfect blessedness.

115b

116a

VIII. Conclusion

Remember all these things, Pythocles; for in this way you will keep far from superstition, and you will be able to under-

116b

[43] For this and the other explanations of meteors, see what has been said about lightning and about comets, secs. 101-2 and 111b above.
[44] See secs. 98b-99a above.

stand phenomena similar to those that have been explained. Above all, devote yourself to the study of primary things and of the infinite, and of what is akin to these, and also to the study of the means of judgment and of your feelings, and to the purpose of all these studies.[45] If these things are thoroughly mastered, they will make it easy to discover the causes of particular phenomena. But those who do not have the firmest possible grasp of these principles would not be able to study the phenomena to advantage, nor would they even understand the reason for which the study is necessary.[46]

[45] The purpose of all is the individual's happiness. The mention of the feelings, by which we tell whether a thing is good or evil for us, leads to the *Letter to Menoeceus,* which treats of the happy life.

[46] In Laertius, between the *Letter to Pythocles* and the *Letter to Menoeceus,* we find: "These were his beliefs in regard to things above the earth. In regard to the manner of life and what we ought to choose and what avoid he wrote as follows—but let us first go through his opinions and those of his followers about the wise man." There then follows a series of short, disconnected, and sometimes contradictory statements about the wise man (secs. 117-21), which Laertius probably found already collected in some Epicurean handbook, and which he obviously added here as an afterthought. At the end he resumes: "Now we must turn to the *Letter.*"

LETTER TO MENOECEUS

I. Introduction

Epicurus to Menoeceus, greeting.

Let no young man delay the study of philosophy, and let no old man become weary of it; for it is never too early nor too late to care for the well-being of the soul. The man who says that the season for this study has not yet come or is already past is like the man who says it is too early or too late for happiness. Therefore, both the young and the old should study philosophy, the former so that as he grows old he may still retain the happiness of youth in his pleasant memories of the past, the latter so that although he is old he may at the same time be young by virtue of his fearlessness of the future. We must therefore study the means of securing happiness, since if we have it we have everything, but if we lack it we do everything in order to gain it.

II. Basic Teachings

A. THE GODS

The gods exist; but it is impious to accept the common beliefs about them. They have no concern with men.[1]

Practice and study without ceasing that which I was always teaching you, being assured that these are the first principles of the good life. After accepting god as the immortal and blessed being depicted by popular opinion, do not ascribe to him anything in addition that is alien to immortality or foreign to blessedness, but rather believe about him whatever can uphold his blessed immortality. The gods do indeed exist, for our perception of them is clear; but they are not such as the crowd imagines them to be, for most men do not retain

[1] See Lucretius, I. 62-135, *et passim.*

the picture of the gods that they first receive.[2] It is not the
man who destroys the gods of popular belief who is impious,
but he who describes the gods in the terms accepted by the
124a many. For the opinions of the many about the gods are not
perceptions but false suppositions.[a] According to these popular suppositions, the gods send great evils to the wicked, great
blessings ⟨to the righteous⟩, for they, being always well dis-
posed to their own virtues, approve those who are like themselves, regarding as foreign all that is different.[3]

B. DEATH

*Philosophy, showing that death is the end of all conscious-
ness, relieves us of all fear of death. A life that is happy is
better than one that is merely long.*[4]

124b Accustom yourself to the belief that death is of no concern
to us, since all good and evil lie in sensation and sensation
ends with death. Therefore the true belief that death is nothing to us makes a mortal life happy, not by adding to it an
infinite time, but by taking away the desire for immortality.
125 For there is no reason why the man who is thoroughly assured
that there is nothing to fear in death should find anything to
fear in life. So, too, he is foolish who says that he fears death,
not because it will be painful when it comes, but because the
anticipation of it is painful; for that which is no burden when
it is present gives pain to no purpose when it is anticipated.
Death, the most dreaded of evils, is therefore of no concern
to us; for while we exist death is not present, and when death
is present we no longer exist. It is therefore nothing either to
the living or to the dead since it is not present to the living,
and the dead no longer are.

But men in general sometimes flee death as the greatest of
evils, sometimes ⟨long for it⟩ as a relief from ⟨the evils⟩ of life.

2 Reading *noousin* with Usener and Bignone, for *nomizousin*.
3 The ambiguous rendition of the last part of this sentence is intentional. "They" may be the gods, who approve men like themselves,
or men, who approve gods. The supplement in the earlier part of this
sentence is by Gassendi.
4 See Lucretius, III. 830-1094.

⟨The wise man neither renounces life⟩ [5] nor fears its end; for living does not offend him, nor does he suppose that not to live is in any way an evil. As he does not choose the food that is most in quantity but that which is most pleasant, so he does not seek the enjoyment of the longest life but of the happiest. 126

He who advises the young man to live well, the old man to die well, is foolish, not only because life is desirable, but also because the art of living well and the art of dying well are one. Yet much worse is he who says that it is well not to have been born, but

once born, be swift to pass through Hades' gates.[6]

If a man says this and really believes it, why does he not depart from life? Certainly the means are at hand for doing so if this really be his firm conviction. If he says it in mockery, he is regarded as a fool among those who do not accept his teaching. 127a

Remember that the future is neither ours nor wholly not ours, so that we may neither count on it as sure to come nor abandon hope of it as certain not to be.

III. The Moral Theory

A. PLEASURE AS THE MOTIVE

The necessary desires are for health of body and peace of mind; if these are satisfied, that is enough for the happy life.

You must consider that of the desires some are natural, some are vain, and of those that are natural, some are necessary, others only natural. Of the necessary desires, some are necessary for happiness, some for the ease of the body, some for life itself. The man who has a perfect knowledge of this will know how to make his every choice or rejection tend toward gaining health of body and peace ⟨of mind⟩, since this is the final end of the blessed life. For to gain this end, namely 127b 128

[5] Supplement by Usener. In Greek the words supplied follow each other.

[6] Theognis, vss. 425, 427.

freedom from pain and fear, we do everything. When once this condition is reached, all the storm of the soul is stilled, since the creature need make no move in search of anything that is lacking, nor seek after anything else to make complete the welfare of the soul and the body. For we only feel the lack of pleasure when from its absence we suffer pain; ⟨but when we do not suffer pain,⟩ [7] we no longer are in need of

129a pleasure. For this reason we say that pleasure is the beginning and the end of the blessed life. We recognize pleasure as the first and natural good; starting from pleasure we accept or reject; and we return to this as we judge every good thing, trusting this feeling of pleasure as our guide.

B. PLEASURES AND PAINS

Pleasure is the greatest good; but some pleasures bring pain, and in choosing, we must consider this.

129b   For the very reason that pleasure is the chief and the natural good, we do not choose every pleasure, but there are times when we pass by pleasures if they are outweighed by the hardships that follow; and many pains we think better than pleasures when a greater pleasure will come to us once we have undergone the long-continued pains. Every pleasure is a good since it has a nature akin to ours; nevertheless, not every pleasure is to be chosen. Just so, every pain is an evil, yet not every pain is of a nature to be avoided on all occa-

130a sions. By measuring and by looking at advantages and disadvantages, it is proper to decide all these things; for under certain circumstances we treat the good as evil, and again, the evil as good.

C. SELF-SUFFICIENCY

The truly wise man is the one who can be happy with a little.

130b   We regard self-sufficiency as a great good, not so that we may enjoy only a few things, but so that, if we do not have many, we may be satisfied with the few, being firmly per-

[7] Supplement by Gassendi.

suaded that they take the greatest pleasure in luxury who regard it as least needed, and that everything that is natural is
easily provided, while vain pleasures are hard to obtain. Indeed, simple sauces bring a pleasure equal to that of lavish
banquets if once the pain due to need is removed; [b] and bread   131a
and water give the greatest pleasure when one who is in need
consumes them. To be accustomed to simple and plain living
is conducive to health and makes a man ready for the necessary tasks of life. It also makes us more ready for the enjoyment of luxury if at intervals we chance to meet with it, and
it renders us fearless against fortune.

D. TRUE PLEASURE

*The truest happiness does not come from enjoyment of
physical pleasures but from a simple life, free from anxiety,
with the normal physical needs satisfied.*

When we say that pleasure is the end, we do not mean the   131b
pleasure of the profligate or that which depends on physical
enjoyment—as some think who do not understand our teachings, disagree with them, or give them an evil interpretation—
but by pleasure we mean the state wherein the body is free
from pain and the mind from anxiety. Neither continual   132a
drinking and dancing, nor sexual love, nor the enjoyment of
fish and whatever else the luxurious table offers brings about
the pleasant life; rather, it is produced by the reason which
is sober, which examines the motive for every choice and rejection, and which drives away all those opinions through
which the greatest tumult lays hold of the mind.

E. PRUDENCE

Prudence or practical wisdom should be our guide.

Of all this the beginning and the chief good is prudence.   132b
For this reason prudence is more precious than philosophy itself. All the other virtues spring from it. It teaches that it is
not possible to live pleasantly without at the same time living
prudently, nobly, and justly, ⟨nor to live prudently, nobly,

and justly⟩ [8] without living pleasantly; for the virtues have
grown up in close union with the pleasant life, and the pleasant life cannot be separated from the virtues.

IV. Conclusion

A. PANEGYRIC ON THE PRUDENT MAN

133   Whom then do you believe to be superior to the prudent
man: he who has reverent opinions about the gods, who is
wholly without fear of death, who has discovered what is the
highest good in life and understands that the highest point in
what is good is easy to reach and hold and that the extreme of
evil is limited either in time or in suffering,[9] and who laughs
at that which some have set up as the ruler of all things,
⟨Necessity? He thinks that the chief power of decision lies
within us, although some things come about by necessity,⟩ [10]
some by chance, and some by our own wills; for he sees that
necessity is irresponsible and chance uncertain, but that our
actions are subject to no power. It is for this reason that our
134   actions merit praise or blame. It would be better to accept the
myth about the gods than to be a slave to the determinism of
the physicists; for the myth hints at a hope for grace through
honors paid to the gods, but the necessity of determinism is in-
escapable. Since the prudent man does not, as do many, regard
chance as a god (for the gods do nothing in disorderly fashion)
or as an unstable cause ⟨of all things⟩,[11] he believes that chance
does ⟨not⟩ [12] give man good and evil to make his life happy or
miserable, but that it does provide opportunities for great
135a   good or evil. Finally, he thinks it better to meet misfortune

---

8 Supplement by Stephanus. See *Principal Doctrines* V; and Cicero,
De Finibus I. 57: "Epicurus declares . . . that it is not possible to live
happily unless one lives wisely, honorably, and justly, nor to live wisely,
honorably, and justly without living happily."

9 See *Principal Doctrines* IV.

10 Bailey has been followed in filling this generally recognized lacuna.

11 Supplement by Bailey.

12 Supplement by Usener.

while acting with reason than to happen upon good fortune while acting senselessly; for it is better that what has been well-planned in our actions ⟨should fail than that what has been ill-planned⟩ [13] should gain success by chance.

B. FINAL WORDS TO MENOECEUS

Meditate on these and like precepts, by day and by night, alone or with a like-minded friend. Then never, either awake or asleep, will you be dismayed; but you will live like a god among men; for life amid immortal blessings is in no way like the life of a mere mortal.   135b

[13] Supplement by Bailey.

PRINCIPAL DOCTRINES ^a

139   I. That which is blessed and immortal is not troubled itself, nor does it cause trouble to another. As a result, it is not
affected by anger or favor, for these belong to weakness.[1]

II. Death is nothing to us; for what has been dissolved has
no sensation, and what has no sensation is nothing to us.

140   III. The removal of all that causes pain marks the boundary of pleasure. Wherever pleasure is present and as long as
it continues, there is neither suffering nor grieving nor both
together.

IV. Continuous bodily suffering does not last long. Intense
pain is very brief, and even pain that barely outweighs physical pleasure does not last many days. Long illnesses permit
physical pleasures that are greater than the pain.

V. It is impossible to live pleasantly without living prudently, well, and justly, ⟨and to live prudently, well, and
justly⟩[2] without living pleasantly. Even though a man live
well and justly, it is not possible for him to live pleasantly if
he lacks that from which stems the prudent life.

141   VI. Any device whatever by which one frees himself from
the fear of others is a natural good.

VII. Some, thinking thus to make themselves safe from
men, wished to become famous and renowned. They won a
natural good if they made their lives secure; but if their lives
were not secure, they did not have that for which, following
the rule of nature, they first sought.

VIII. No pleasure is evil in itself; but the means by which

---

[1] Scholium: "In other places he says that the gods are to be discerned
by reason; some of them exist according to number, others exist in
human form from the constant and uniform flow of similar atoms sent
to the same spot."

[2] Supplied by Gassendi. The text of this *Doctrine* is very uncertain.

certain pleasures are gained bring pains many times greater than the pleasures.

IX. If every pleasure were cumulative, and if this were the case both in time and in regard to the whole or the most important parts of our nature, then pleasures would not differ from each other.   142

X. If the things that produce the pleasures of the dissolute were able to drive away from their minds their fears about what is above them and about death and pain, and to teach them the limit of desires, we would have no reason to find fault with the dissolute; for they would fill themselves with pleasure from every source and would be free from pain and sorrow, which are evil.

XI. If our dread of the phenomena above us, our fear lest death concern us, and our inability to discern the limits of pains and desires were not vexatious to us, we would have no need of the natural sciences.

XII. It is not possible for one to rid himself of his fears about the most important things if he does not understand the nature of the universe but dreads some of the things he has learned in the myths. Therefore, it is not possible to gain unmixed happiness without natural science.   143

XIII. It is of no avail to prepare security against other men while things above us and beneath the earth and in the whole infinite universe in general are still dreaded.

XIV. When reasonable security from men has been attained, then the security that comes from peace of mind and withdrawal from the crowd is present, sufficient in strength and most unmixed in well-being.[3]

XV. Natural wealth is limited and easily obtained; the wealth defined by vain fancies is always beyond reach.   144

XVI. Fortune seldom troubles the wise man. Reason has controlled his greatest and most important affairs, controls them throughout his life, and will continue to control them.

XVII. The just man is least disturbed; the unjust man is filled with the greatest turmoil.

[3] The text of this *Doctrine* is very uncertain.

XVIII. When once the pain caused by need has been removed, bodily pleasure will not be increased in amount but
only varied in quality. The mind attains its utmost pleasure
in reflecting on the very things that used to cause the greatest mental fears and on things like them.

145   XIX. Time that is unlimited and time that is limited afford
equal pleasure if one measures pleasure's extent by reason.

XX. The flesh believes that pleasure is limitless and that
it requires unlimited time; but the mind, understanding the
end and limit of the flesh and ridding itself of fears of the
future, secures a complete life and has no longer any need for
unlimited time. It does not, however, avoid pleasure; and
when circumstances bring on the end of life, it does not depart as if it still lacked any portion of the good life.

146   XXI. The man who understands the limits of living knows
that it is easy to obtain that which removes the pain caused
by want and that which perfects the whole life. Therefore, he
has no need of things that involve struggle.

XXII. It is necessary to take into account the real purpose
of knowledge and all the evidence of that clear perception to
which we refer our opinions. If we do not, all will be full of
bad judgment and confusion.

XXIII. If you struggle against all your sensations, you will
have no standard of comparison by which to measure even the
sensations you judge false.

147   XXIV. If you reject any sensation, and if you fail to distinguish between conjecture based upon that which awaits
confirmation and evidence given by the senses, by the feelings,
and by the mental examinations of confirmed concepts,[4] you
will confuse the other sensations with unfounded conjecture
and thus destroy the whole basis for judgment. If among all
opinions you accept as equally valid both those that await
confirmation and those that have been confirmed, you will not
free yourself from error, since you will have preserved all the
uncertainty about every judgment of what is true and what
is not true.[b]

148   XXV. If you do not at all times refer each of your actions

4 See *Life of Epicurus* 31a, and notes.

to the natural end,[5] but fall short of this and turn aside to something else in choosing and avoiding, your deeds will not agree with your words.

XXVI. Those desires that do not bring pain if they are not satisfied are not necessary; and they are easily thrust aside whenever to satisfy them appears difficult or likely to cause injury.

XXVII. Of the things that wisdom prepares for insuring lifelong happiness, by far the greatest is the possession of friends.

XXVIII. The same wisdom that permits us to be confident that no evil is eternal or even of long duration also recognizes that in our limited state the security that can be most perfectly gained is that of friendship.

XXIX. Of the desires, some are natural ⟨and necessary; some are natural⟩ [6] but not necessary; and others are neither natural nor necessary but arise from empty opinion.[7]   149

XXX. Among the bodily desires, those rest on empty opinion that are eagerly pursued although if unsatisfied they bring no pain. That they are not got rid of is because of man's empty opinion, not because of their own nature.

XXXI. Natural justice is a compact resulting from expediency by which men seek to prevent one man from injuring others and to protect him from being injured by them.[8]   150

XXXII. There is no such thing as justice or injustice among those beasts that cannot make agreements not to injure or be injured. This is also true of those tribes that are unable or unwilling to make agreements not to injure or be injured.

XXXIII. There is no such thing as justice in the abstract; it

[5] That is, to pleasure.

[6] Supplement added by Bignone.

[7] Scholium: "Epicurus thought that those desires were natural and necessary that relieve pain, as drink for the thirsty; that those were natural but not necessary that give variety to pleasure although not needed for removing pain, for example, extravagance in food; and that desires for such things as crowns and the dedication of statues were neither natural nor necessary."

[8] With *Principal Doctrines* XXXI and XXXVI, compare Lucretius, V. 1010-27.

is merely a compact between men in their various relations with each other, in whatever circumstances they may be, that they will neither injure nor be injured.

151 XXXIV. Injustice is not evil in itself, but only in the fear and apprehension that one will not escape those who have been set up to punish the offense.

XXXV. If a man has secretly violated any of the terms of the mutual compact not to injure or be injured, he cannot feel confident that he will be undetected in the future even if he has escaped ten thousand times in the past; for until his death it will remain uncertain whether he will escape.

XXXVI. In general, justice is the same for all, a thing found useful by men in their relations with each other; but it does not follow that it is the same for all in each individual place and circumstance.

152 XXXVII. Among the things commonly held just, that which has proved itself useful in men's mutual relationships has the stamp of justice whether or not it be the same for all; if anyone makes a law and it does not prove useful in men's relationships with each other, it is no longer just in its essence. If, however, the law's usefulness in the matter of justice should change and it should meet men's expectations only for a short time, nonetheless during that short time it was just in the eyes of those who look simply at facts and do not confuse themselves with empty words.

153 XXXVIII. If, although no new circumstances have arisen, those things that were commonly held just in these matters did not in their actual effects correspond with that conception, they were not just. Whenever, as a result of new circumstances, the same things that had been regarded as just were no longer useful, they were just at the time when they were useful for the relations of citizens to each other; but afterwards, when they were no longer useful, they were no longer just.

154 XXXIX. He who has best controlled his lack of confidence in the face of external forces has, as far as possible, treated these externals as akin to himself or, when that was impossi-

ble, at least as not alien. Where he was not able to do even this, he kept to himself and avoided whatever it was best to avoid.[9]

XL. Those who were best able to prepare security for themselves in relation to their neighbors [10] lived most pleasantly with their neighbors since they had the most perfect assurance; and enjoying the most complete intimacy, they did not lament the death of one who died before his time as if it were an occasion for sorrow.

[9] Another *Doctrine* of which the text is very bad. The meaning is obscure, but the general sense seems to be that the prudent man gains security from external dangers by winning friends where he can, and by avoiding those whose friendship he cannot gain.

[10] That is, those who were most self-sufficient and least dependent upon others.

IV. Every pain is easily disregarded; for that which is intense is of brief duration, and the suffering brought by a physical pain that lasts long is slight.[1]

VII. For a wrongdoer to be undetected is difficult; and for him to have confidence that his concealment will continue is impossible.[2]

IX. Necessity is an evil; but there is no necessity for continuing to live subject to necessity.[3]

XI. Most men are in a coma when they are at rest and mad when they act.

XIV. We have been born once and there can be no second birth. For all eternity we shall no longer be. But you, although you are not master of tomorrow, are postponing your happiness. We waste away our lives in delaying, and each of us dies without having enjoyed leisure.[4]

XV. As if they were our own handiwork, we place a high value on our characters whether or not we are virtuous and praised by other men. So, too, we should regard the characters of those about us if they are our friends.[5]

XVI. No one chooses a thing realizing that it is evil; but when it appears as good in contrast to a greater evil, he takes the bait and is caught.

XVII. We should not regard the young man as happy, but rather the old man whose life has been fortunate. The young man at the height of his power is often baffled by fortune and

---

1 See *Principal Doctrines* IV, of which this is a condensation.

2 See *Principal Doctrines* XXXV, of which this is a condensation.

3 See Seneca, *Letters* I. 12. 10 (Usener, No. 487).

4 "Leisure" and "happiness" both refer to the life of the Epicurean sage. Since a single person is addressed in the third sentence, this *Saying* probably comes from a letter of Epicurus.

5 The text and meaning of this *Saying* are both doubtful.

driven from his course; but the old man has come to anchor in age as in a harbor, and holds in sure and happy memory blessings for which once he could scarcely hope.

XVIII. If sight, association, and intercourse are removed, the passion of love is ended.

XIX. He has become an old man on the day on which he forgot his past blessings.[6]

XXI. We must not resist Nature but obey her. We shall obey her if we satisfy the necessary desires and also those bodily desires that do not harm us while sternly rejecting those that are harmful.[7]

XXIII. Every friendship in itself is to be desired; but the first cause of friendship was a man's needs.

XXIV. Dreams have neither divine nature nor prophetic power, but they are the result of idols that impinge upon us.[8]

XXV. Poverty, if in proper proportion to the natural purposes of life, is great wealth; but the wealth that is unlimited is great poverty.[9]

XXVI. One must assume that the long argument and the short tend to the same end.[10]

XXVII. The benefits of other pursuits come to those who have reached the end of a difficult course, but in the study of philosophy pleasure keeps pace with growing knowledge; for pleasure does not follow learning; rather, learning and pleasure advance side by side.

XXVIII. Those who are hasty in making friends are not to be approved; nor yet should you commend those who avoid friendship, for risks must be run for its sake.

XXIX. To speak frankly, I would prefer as I study nature to speak in oracles that which is of advantage to all men even though it be understood by none, rather than to conform to

[6] By contrast, the Epicurean sage remains young by remembering the happiness of the past.

[7] See *Principal Doctrines* XXVI and XXIX.

[8] See Lucretius, IV. 962-1036.

[9] See Lucretius, V. 1117-19; Seneca, *Letters* IV. 10 (Usener, No. 477).

[10] The text is clear, but without a context this *Saying* is pointless.

popular opinion and thus gain the praise that is scattered broadcast by the many.

XXXI. It is possible to provide security against other ills, but as far as death is concerned, we men all live in a city without walls.[11]

XXXII. The honor paid to a wise man is a great good for those who honor him.[12]

XXXIII. The voice of the flesh bids us escape from hunger, thirst, and cold; for he who is free of these and expects to remain so might vie in happiness even with Zeus.

XXXIV. We do not so much need the help of our friends as the confidence of their help in need.[13]

XXXV. Do not spoil what you have by desiring what you have not; but remember that what you now have was once among the things only hoped for.

XXXVII. When confronted by evil the soul is weak, but not when faced with good; for pleasures make the soul secure but pains ruin it.

XXXVIII. He is of very small account who sees many good reasons for ending his life.

XXXIX. Neither he who is always seeking material aid from his friends nor he who never thinks of such aid as possible is a true friend; for the one engages in petty trade, taking a favor instead of gratitude, and the other deprives himself of hope for the future.[14]

XL. He who says that all things happen by necessity can hardly find fault with the one who denies that all happens by necessity; for on his own theory this very argument is voiced by necessity.

---

[11] Some ancient writers quote these words as by Metrodorus, a follower of Epicurus.

[12] The text of this *Saying* is quite uncertain.

[13] The fact that the same Greek word can mean either "need" or "help" makes possible a play on words that is only suggested by the English "need the help" and "help in need."

[14] See XXIII above for the idea that mutual utility is an essential part of friendship.

XLI. At one and the same time we must laugh, philosophize, manage our business, and carry out our other duties, while never ceasing to shout out the words of the true philosophy.

XLII. The time of the beginning of the greatest good and the time of its enjoyment are one.[15]

XLIII. To love money unjustly gained is evil, and to love money justly gained is shameful; for sordid niggardliness is unseemly even when accompanied by justice [or even in the case of a just man].

XLIV. The wise man who has become accustomed to limited means knows better how to share with others than how to take from them, so great a treasure of self-sufficiency has he found.

XLV. The study of nature does not produce men who are fond of boasting and shouting or who make a show of that culture that is highly prized by the many, but rather men who are haughty [16] and self-sufficient, and who take pride in the high qualities that depend upon themselves and not in those that depend on their possessions.

XLVI. Let us completely banish our evil habits as if they were evil men who have done us long and grievous harm.

XLVIII. While we are on the journey of life, we must try to make what is before us better than what is past; but when we come to the journey's end, we must be content and calm.

LI. I understand from you that your natural disposition is too much inclined toward sexual passion. Follow your inclination as you will provided only that you neither violate the laws, disturb well-established customs, harm any one of your neighbors, injure your own body, nor waste your possessions. That you be not checked by some one of these provisos is

---

[15] The "greatest good" is pleasure, which here is called complete from the beginning. This neglects the happiness of memory, on which Epicurus laid great stress.

[16] Bailey and Bignone retain the manuscript reading, *sobarous*, which I translate. Usener reads *aphobous*, "fearless"; Gomperz, *athorubous*, "unperturbed"; and Leopold, *asobarous*, "modest."

impossible; for a man never gets any good from sexual passion, and he is fortunate if he does not receive harm.[17]

LII. Friendship dances through the world bidding us all to awaken to the recognition of happiness [or to awaken and give thanks].

LIII. Envy no man. The good do not merit envy. As for the evil, the greater their good fortune, the greater the pains that they inflict upon themselves.

LIV. It is not the pretended but the real pursuit of philosophy that is needed; for we do not need to seem to enjoy good health but to enjoy it in truth.

LV. We should find solace for misfortune in the happy memory of the things that are gone and in the knowledge that what has come to be cannot be undone.

LVIII. We must free ourselves from the prison of private and public business.

LIX. What cannot be satisfied is not a man's belly, as men think, but rather his false idea about the unending filling of his belly.

LX. Every man passes out of life as if he had just been born.[18]

LXII. If the anger of parents against their children is justified, it is quite foolish for the children to resist it and to fail to seek forgiveness. If the anger is not justified but is unreasonable, it is folly for a child to increase the unreasoning wrath by his own anger and not to try to turn it aside in other directions by a display of good feeling.[19]

[17] This seems to be from a letter of Epicurus in reply to one from a follower.

[18] This seemingly straightforward *Saying* has been interpreted in many ways: "A man leaves life no better than he entered it" (Seneca); "Our condition after death will be as it was before birth" (Usener); "We brought nothing into the world and can take nothing out of it" (Bignone); "Life is so brief that every man at his death is like a new-born child" (Bailey).

[19] The text is very doubtful in several places, but the general meaning seems clear.

LXIII. There is also a limit in simple living. He who fails to heed this limit falls into an error as great as that of the man who gives way to extravagance.

LXIV. We should welcome praise from others if it comes unsought, but we should be concerned with correcting ourselves.

LXV. It is folly for a man to pray to the gods for that which he has the power to obtain by himself.

LXVI. We show our feeling for friends, not by wailing, but by meditating.[20]

LXVII. Since the attainment of riches can scarcely be accomplished without servitude to crowds or kings, a free life cannot obtain much wealth, but such a life has all possessions in unfailing supply. Should such a life happen to fall upon great wealth, this too it can so distribute as to gain the good will of those about.[21]

LXVIII. Nothing satisfies him to whom what is enough is little.[22]

LXIX. The thankless nature of the soul makes the creature endlessly greedy of changes in its way of life.[23]

LXX. Do nothing while you live that will cause you to fear if it becomes known to your neighbor.

LXXI. Test each of your desires by this question: "What will happen to me if that which this desire seeks is brought to fulfillment, and what if it is not?"

LXXIII. That we have suffered certain bodily pains aids us in guarding against their like.

LXXIV. In a philosophical dispute, he gains most who is defeated, since he learns most.

[20] That is, not by wailing at their funerals but by meditating on their lives.

[21] For the idea that freedom and self-sufficiency go hand in hand, see LXXVII below.

[22] This may be a corruption of words quoted by Aelian in *Varia Historia* IV. 13 (Usener, No. 473): "He who is not satisfied with a little is never satisfied."

[23] See LIX above.

LXXV. The saying, "Observe the end of a long life," shows small thanks for past good fortune.[24]

LXXVI. As you grow old you are such as I urge you to be, and you have recognized the difference between studying philosophy for yourself and for Greece. I rejoice with you.[25]

LXXVII. Freedom is the greatest fruit of self-sufficiency.[26]

LXXVIII. The noble man is chiefly concerned with wisdom and friendship; of these, the former is a mortal good, the latter an immortal one.

LXXIX. He who is calm disturbs neither himself nor another.[27]

LXXX. The first step toward salvation is to watch over one's youth and to guard against that which stains everything by maddening desires.

LXXXI. The soul neither rids itself of confusion nor gains a joy worthy of the name through the possession of greatest wealth and of the honor and admiration bestowed by the common crowd, or through any of the other things sought by unlimited desire.

[24] The commoner form of the proverb, "Call no man happy until he is dead," would make clearer the point of this *Saying*. The Epicurean even in an unfortunate old age should still be happy in the memory of better days that are gone.

[25] Epicurean philosophy was to be proclaimed to the world.

[26] See LXVII above.

[27] See *Principal Doctrines* I.

APPENDIX NOTES

APPENDIX NOTES

Introduction

Note *a*, p. ix. The standard collection of the remaining works of these philosophers is Hermann Diels, *Die Fragmente der Vorsokratiker* (3 vols., 10th edn. by Walter Kranz, Berlin, 1960-65). A chapter is devoted to each philosopher, and as a rule each chapter consists of two parts: A, which contains the ancient testimony in regard to his life and teachings; and B, which contains the actual fragments, usually passages quoted by other ancient writers in works now extant, occasionally bits that have been preserved on papyrus. The *testimonia*, which are usually much more voluminous than the fragments, are given only in the original Greek or Latin; but the fragments are given both in Greek and in a German translation. References to this work are by chapter, part of chapter, and number, e.g., 22 A 12, or 56 B 3. Kathleen Freeman's *Ancilla* (Cambridge, Mass., 1948) contains an English translation of the fragments and preserves Diels's numbering. G. S. Kirk and J. E. Raven, in their *Presocratic Philosophers* (Cambridge, England, 1957), have translated and discussed the more important of the *testimonia* and fragments, and have combined this into a history of Greek philosophy before Socrates that is very complete and scholarly. Unfortunately, it is exceedingly difficult to use, since they have introduced a new system for numbering the *testimonia* and the fragments, with the result that there is no simple way to locate their translation of a passage referred to in another modern book. Other standard books on early Greek philosophy are J. Burnet, *Early Greek Philosophy* (4th edn.; London, 1930), with translation of much of the important evidence and full citations, and C. Bailey, *Greek Atomists and Epicurus* (Oxford, 1928), dealing primarily with Epicurus but containing long chapters on Leucippus and Democritus and brief notices of their predecessors. Bailey has shorter accounts of the development of Greek physical philosophy in the introductions to his editions of the works of Epicurus (Oxford, 1926) and of Lucretius (3 vols.; Oxford, 1947). For a discussion of works on the pre-Socratics between 1945 and 1954, see Minar, *Classical Weekly*, XLVII (1953-54), 161-70, 177-82.

Life of Epicurus

Note *a*, p. 6. The first three terms—sensations, concepts, and feelings—are relatively clear in themselves and will be explained in what immediately follows. The phrase translated "mental apprehension of appearances," which is not explained here or elsewhere in extant Epicurean material, presents real difficulty. As will be clear from what follows (see also Lucretius, IV. 722-822), all thought is regarded as a process of visualization. In the simplest case the mind pictures what the senses send to it. The mind can also be stirred to visualization by emanations too subtle to affect the senses. All the emanations may be misleading, and it is only by the purposeful application of the mind to them that the truth can be discovered. The mind can store up these mental images or concepts, however gained, and can use them to identify, classify, and test new sensations and images (see sec. 33a). So far, all is quite certain, but the mental apprehension of appearances seems to involve more than this. Apparently the mind can combine these concepts, which depend on emanations from material things (see the next-to-last sentence of sec. 32), and form new concepts of phenomena that can never have given off emanations of any sort at any time; for example, the two basic elements of Epicurean physics, void and the atom (see Lucretius, II. 737-45, 1044-47). Our phrase then would include the application of the mind to these new concepts, and might be freely rendered, "the mental examination of scientific concepts" (Bailey, *Epicurus*, p. 274). The problem is discussed at length by Bailey in his *Greek Atomists and Epicurus*, pp. 559-76; and with quite different conclusions by DeWitt in his *Epicurus*, pp. 133-54.

Note *b*, p. 7. It is necessary to the materialistic concept of thought that even such visions be true representations of idols or emanations, but the idols themselves may be false, formed in the air spontaneously or by combinations of other idols or their parts, or strayed from another time and place (see Lucretius, IV. 722-48). When the mind is off its guard in sleep or delirium, these isolated and distorted idols may be accepted at their face value, but normally they are recognized for what they are and are rejected (see Lucretius, IV. 749-67).

Note *c*, p. 7. The square tower that appears round when seen from a distance was a favorite illustration of the problem awaiting solution by a clear and near view (see Lucretius, IV. 353-63, 501).

Letter to Herodotus

Note *a*, p. 9. Much of the difficulty of the letter doubtless arises from this fact. It was composed not to introduce beginners to the system, but to refresh the minds of those who had once mastered it.

Note *b*, p. 9. The most important matters beyond the reach of the senses are the basic elements in the universe (atoms and void) and the gods. The former by their nature cannot send off emanations; the emanations from the gods are so subtle that they cannot be perceived by the senses but pass directly to the mind.

Note *c*, p. 10. To the Epicureans, change was the same as destruction. See the often-repeated lines in Lucretius: "For whenever a thing is changed and departs from its proper limits, that is at once the death of that which was before" (I. 670-71, 792-93, II. 753-54, III. 519-20).

Note *d*, p. 11. Between this sentence and the next we need, in order to complete the logical development, a statement that there can be nothing outside the whole to define its edge, and therefore the whole can have no edge. The whole argument can be criticized for assuming a false identity between "boundless" and "infinite." For example, the surface of a sphere is boundless but it is not infinite.

Note *e*, p. 13. Three states of matter—solid, liquid, and gas—are here explained. The atoms that fly far apart after collisions form gases; those that are closely entangled but continue to vibrate within narrow limits form solids; and those that, although not entangled themselves, have their motions limited by a surface film of interwoven atoms form liquids. See Lucretius, II. 80-141. Here and in the second sentence below, Epicurus assumes that even within a solid each atom is surrounded by void.

Note *f*, p. 13. Literally "solidity" or "firmness." In Epicurean physics, when atoms of different masses collide, they recoil and change their directions, but each continues to move at its original "atomic" velocity. Actually if two elastic bodies of different masses but the same velocity collide and recoil, the total energy of the system remains the same except for energy lost as heat, but the velocity as well as the direction of each body will be changed.

Note *g*, p. 14. This is a good example of Epicurean proof by noncontradiction. If a theory explains a given set of phenomena and is not contradicted by the available evidence, it may be accepted, at least tentatively. In the absence of carefully controlled experiments, this sometimes led to fantastic results—but the method of modern science is not very different.

Note *h*, p. 14. The text of this sentence is uncertain and its meaning is not clear. According to Epicurean kinetics, the atoms move with a velocity greater than that of light (see Lucretius, II. 142-64), maintaining this even when they are entangled in a solid object. Within such an object, however, they are in constant collision, and their motions are in all directions. If the object moves, its motion may be thought of as the effective sum of all the conflicting motions of its atoms. Moreover, its motions will be hindered by collisions between its own atoms (which are inconceivably many) and the free atoms in space. We are apparently to think of the idol as a film, one atom deep, with wide spaces between the atoms. If all the atoms in the film are moving in one direction (which seems to be assumed), and if most of the atoms that it meets pass through it without contact, its speed will almost equal that of the freely moving atoms (see Lucretius, IV. 176-215 and VI. 343-44).

Note *i*, p. 16. The idols coming from sensible objects act upon our eyes, which in turn affect the mind. The idols of subtler nature, coming from things that are imperceptible, act directly on the mind. In either case, the rapid succession of separate idols creates a single continuous picture of the object and its qualities. Although the idols come from the outer surface of objects, their speed is due to the unceasing action of the atoms within the solid, and in some way the "quality" of the idol (perhaps this means its appearance of solidity) is controlled by this interior atomic activity.

Note *j*, p. 16. The important word in this sentence is "purposeful." We can trust the intent look, not the casual glance, and concentrated thinking, not mental wandering. In the last clause, the "continuous impact of idols" causes sight, and the "impression left by one," thought.

Note *k*, p. 18. A sensible object may be so treated that it loses its secondary qualities such as color, hardness, etc., and its particular shape and size; but it will always retain the three basic qualities—it will always have some shape, size, and mass. (The last two are not mentioned by Epicurus, but may be easily understood.) These properties, which can never be completely lost, are the only ones possessed by the atoms, and, as he says in the next sentence, these are enough to cause the differences in objects.

Note *l*, p. 19. Any part that can be divided must in Epicurean physics contain void, and therefore it must be soft. Since from soft first beginnings nothing hard can be made (see Lucretius, I. 565-76), all things would be soft.

Note *m*, p. 19. As in the paradox of Achilles and the tortoise. This difficult sentence seems to make what is essentially the same point in two different ways: we cannot assume infinite divisibility of the particles of matter in any sensible object; and in material things, we cannot assume an infinitely diminishing series. Bailey translates the sentence as follows:

> Therefore, we must not only do away with division into smaller and smaller parts to infinity, in order that we may not make all things weak, and so in the composition of aggregate bodies be compelled to crush and squander the things that exist into the non-existent, but we must not either suppose that in limited bodies there is a possibility of continuing to infinity in passing ever to smaller and smaller parts.

Hicks, in the Loeb edition of Diogenes Laertius, *Lives,* has the following:

> Hence not only must we reject as impossible subdivision *ad infinitum* into smaller and smaller parts, lest we make all things too weak and, in our conceptions of the aggregates, be driven to pulverize the things that exist, *i.e.* the atoms, and annihilate them; but in dealing with finite things we must also reject as impossible the progression *ad infinitum* by less and less increments.

Note *n*, p. 21. The text is somewhat doubtful, and my translation, "the least perceptible parts of sensible things," is a considerable expansion of any word that has been conjectured; but the sense of the passage is certain. Since the last half of the sentence marks a single point of difference between the least visible parts (which, of course, can have separate existence even though we may not be able to see them separately) and the atom's least parts (which cannot exist separately), the first part of the sentence must refer to that which the two kinds of least parts have in common.

Note *o*, p. 21. Each Epicurean world is flat, and is oriented as is our own. Motion extending upward from us will come to the feet of those in worlds above us, and motion downward to the heads of those below. Motion that is upward for us is therefore upward for all the worlds, and motion down is down. However ridiculous this paragraph may sound to us, it follows the Epicurean principle of trusting the evidence of the senses. The direction that our senses call down *is* down, and that is the end of the matter.

Note *p*, p. 22. Here and in the next sentence "weight" represents the Greek word which was translated "mass" in sec. 54 and also in the scholium given in note 18 (p. 13). Epicurus does not distinguish between mass, the property of a body which resists any change in its state of motion or rest, and weight, which results from the action of gravity upon a body's mass and causes a free body to move with constant acceleration toward the center of the earth. If we assume for the atoms an initial motion downward, mass will cause this motion to continue without acceleration, but mass cannot be the cause of the atoms' downward motion, nor can it account for the tendency of an atom to return to its original downward motion after it has been deflected. Weight would account both for the original downward motion and for the return to motion in that direction; but motion downward caused by weight would be subject to constant acceleration. Epicurus may have visualized the atoms' uniform downward motion in terms of raindrops falling in parallel lines at a constant velocity, but their velocity is constant only because they are falling through air and have reached their terminal velocity in that medium long before they are close to the earth.

Note *q*, p. 22. Although a collision does not reduce the velocity of the atom, it does change or even reverse its direction, thus reducing the net distance covered. In the extreme case of a solid at rest, the velocity of each atom vibrating in its own bit of void within the solid is the same as that of an atom moving freely in space; but the net distance it covers may be zero.

Note *r*, p. 22. We have a contrast here between the shortest length of time recognizable by the senses, in which a compound body (and the atoms of which it is composed) may be seen to move from one point to another, and a period of time appreciable only by the reason, in which each atom is moving with its characteristic velocity, each in its own direction, and the body as a whole makes no detectable motion. In the next such period many of the atoms will have changed their directions because of collisions. As far as concerns transfer from place to place, the net movement of an atom in a given time will be the resultant of all its conflicting motions; and the net movement of the whole solid will be the resultant of all the motions of all its atoms. In this way it can be said that the collisions bring the motion within reach of our senses (see sec. 47a, which is printed following sec. 62; see also Lucretius' discussion of the magnet, VI. 999-1041).

Note *s*, p. 23. Must we suppose that, if the atoms individually move in every direction while the whole body moves from *A* to *B*, the whole body has also moved in all these directions? No; for if this were true, when the body comes to *B* we would be conscious of its motion, not from the direction of *A*, but from some other direction, the last in which it had been moving. This is not a very serious objection, nor a very serious answer. If we are to follow the previous reasoning, at any point in time the whole body should have a motion equal to the resultant of the motions of all its atoms at that particular time; but, in the case of a body composed of a large number of atoms, we can assume that this resultant motion would be in the same direction and at the same rate as the motion of the whole would be in an appreciable length of time.

Note *t*, p. 23. In Lucretius, III. 136-46, there is a distinction between the *anima*, "spirit," scattered through the whole body, and the *animus,* "mind," concentrated in the breast. The *animus* is a part of the *anima,* and the latter term sometimes includes both. This distinction seems to have been normal in the Epicurean school and quite certainly goes back to Epicurus himself. See the scholium at the end of sec. 66, and also the following from Aetius, IV. 4: "Epicurus believed that the soul was in two parts with the reason seated in the breast and the unreasoning part distributed through the whole body" (Usener, No. 312).

Note *u,* p. 23. In Lucretius, III. 231-57, we have, as here, an unknown element in the soul; but in addition to this there are in Lucretius three elements, not two, and these are said to *be* air, breath (i.e., air in motion), and heat rather than merely to *resemble* them. In distinguishing between air and breath Lucretius seems to present the usual teaching of the Epicureans. See, for example, Aetius, IV. 3: "The soul is a mixture of four things: one like fire, one like air, one like breath, and a fourth element without a name" (Usener, No. 315).

Note *v,* p. 29. Three types of worlds are supposed in the lacuna. Worlds of the first type always contain the seeds from which living things can be formed. In those of the second type, such seeds may be present or they may be lacking, apparently as chance dictates. In those of the third type, these seeds are never found. Since no one can prove the existence of worlds of either of the last types, Epicurus concludes that all the worlds that exist are of the same general type as the one world that we know, just as all the animals in a flock tend to be like the one we see and identify as, for example, a sheep.

Note *w,* p. 32. Bailey translates this sentence thus: "If, therefore, we think that a phenomenon probably occurs in some such particular way, and that in circumstances under which it is equally possible for us to be at peace, when we realize that it may occur in several ways, we shall be just as little disturbed as if we know that it occurs in some particular way." Hicks's rendering is: "If then we think that an event could happen in one or other particular way out of several, we shall be as tranquil when we recognize that it actually comes about in more ways than one as if we knew that it happens in this particular way."

Letter to Pythocles

Note *a*, p. 37. A more or less globular form with three projecting angles is possible, but there can be no such thing as a triangular solid. (Note that he is describing the world, which must have three dimensions, not the earth, which might be a plane.) But probably Epicurus is thinking of a tetrahedron, a solid with four faces, each of them a triangle, and four angles. For the possible shapes of the world, see *Letter to Herodotus* 74a, and scholium.

Note *b*, p. 38. The views attacked were held by Leucippus and/or Democritus (see Bailey, *Atomists,* pp. 90-101, 138-48; Kirk and Raven, pp. 409-14). This paragraph may also be translated: "It is not enough that there be a gathering of matter and a whirl in an empty space in which it is possible for a world to come into being (from necessity as some think) and to grow until it strikes another world (as one of our so-called physicists says); for this contradicts the things that we see."

Note *c*, p. 38. Our senses, of course, can give us no evidence in regard to the formation of the heavenly bodies, but they do tell us of earthly phenomena that may suggest the manner of their formation. For example, place water and a little sand in a bowl and give it a rotary motion setting up an eddy in the water. The sand will gather in the center and the water (the lighter of the two) will rise on the sides, the cross section of the whole approximating that of the lower part of a sphere. If still lighter elements like fire and air were in the whirl, we might suppose that they would rise still higher, continuing the curve until they met at the top, the whole forming a hollow sphere. Going one step further, we can imagine new eddies set up by the lighter elements in the upper part of the sphere with the fire concentrated in the center of each eddy. Here we have a small model of the creation of a world, based on the evidence of the senses or at least not contradicted by them (!).

Note *d*, p. 39. As far as our senses are concerned, the sun is the size it appears to be, that is, our senses report correctly the size of the image that reaches them. But we do not have a near view, and there is the possibility that the image has been distorted, as was the image of the square tower that seemed round at a distance (*Life of Epicurus* 34a, and note). In either case, we have a problem awaiting confirmation. We get this confirmation in the case of the tower by a near view, which shows the shape of the tower beyond question. In the case of the sun, this near view is impossible and we must be content with analogies from the appearance of distant fires on earth. From these we conclude that the real size of the sun is not very different from its apparent size.

Note *e*, p. 39. See Lucretius, V. 509-33, 650-79. There are three apparent motions to be explained: (1) the daily rising and setting of the heavenly bodies; (2) the delay of the sun and the moon relative to the motion of the zodiac—such that, if we think of the stars as setting the standard, the sun loses about four minutes a day or one day a year, and the moon about forty minutes a day or one day in a lunar month—and the more complex motions of the planets; and (3) the spiral motion of the sun's orbit that makes the sun cross the sky higher and higher each day from midwinter to midsummer and then move back again during the other half of the year, the orbits of the moon and the planets showing somewhat similar but more complicated patterns. Epicurus discusses the first of these motions in the early part of this section before the lacuna; and in the last part, beginning with the first complete sentence after the lacuna, he is trying to explain the third. Reasons for the second element in the motions may have been given in the passage that is lost; in any case, Epicurus returns to this problem in sec. 114a.

Note *f*, p. 45. In Greek, as in Latin, there are words for lightning and for thunder, and also a third word, conventionally translated "thunderbolt," meaning "lightning that strikes."

Note *g*, p. 45. Apparently we are to think of many eddies of wind crowding together and bursting into flame. These flames push horizontally against the clouds, which are thus more and more closely compressed, until finally a portion of fire detaches itself from the rest and plunges downward. This explanation differs from the one that follows only in its first stage. Here we start with wind that bursts into flame, there with fire particles already in the clouds.

Note *h*, p. 47. Reading *eäri* with Usener. The manuscripts give *aëri*, "in the air." The two sentences ending here have been translated quite freely, in an effort to express an acceptable meaning. Hicks translates them as follows: "Or again, by congelation in clouds which have uniform density a fall of snow might occur through the clouds which contain moisture being densely packed in close proximity to each other; and these clouds produce a sort of compression and cause hail, and this happens mostly in spring." Bailey translates: "Or else owing to congelation in clouds of uniform thinness an exudation of this kind might arise from watery clouds lying side by side and rubbing against one another; for they produce hail by causing coagulation, a process most frequent in the atmosphere."

Note *i*, p. 47. This sentence seems to be an afterthought. He has said that snow falls when clouds rub together as they freeze, and hail, if clouds already frozen are subject to pressure. He now adds that if such frozen clouds rub together the result is the same as if the freezing and the rubbing were simultaneous, namely, a fall of snow.

Note *j*, p. 51. The outer edge of a vortex was supposed to move with greater angular velocity than the portions nearer the center. The first explanation, then, assumes that the stars, which make 366 circuits of the earth while the sun makes 365, are more distant than the sun. The moon is much nearer than the earth, and the planets are at varying distances. The third explanation apparently assumes that the actual velocity of the bodies is the same, and that therefore the ones that are the most distant have the lowest angular velocity and appear to us to move most slowly. In the second explanation, there is one force that tends to carry all the bodies at the same angular velocity about the earth, but some of the bodies have a natural tendency to move in the opposite direction, which delays them.

Letter to Menoeceus

Note *a*, p. 54. From the gods, as from all else that exists, a constant stream of idols flows. These idols of the gods are so tenuous that they affect the mind but not the sense of sight. A series of these idols builds up in the mind a true concept of the divine nature. The wise man's belief about the gods is based on his deliberate apprehension of this mental concept; the belief of the many is a supposition, in which the original concept is obscured by the additions of opinion.

Note *b*, p. 57. One of the basic teachings of Epicurus was that when the natural needs of the body have been satisfied, bodily pleasures cannot be increased in quantity although they may be varied in quality. See *Principal Doctrines* XVIII.

Principal Doctrines

Note *a*, p. 60. After the *Letter to Menoeceus,* Laertius adds the statement that Epicurus rejected divination, and then discusses the differences between the ethical teachings of the Epicureans and of the Cyrenaics, who made sensual pleasure the highest good. He then ends his biography of Epicurus by giving the forty so-called *Principal Doctrines (Kuriai Doxai,* variously translated as "Principal Doctrines," "Chief Sayings,"

"Sovereign Maxims"; called by Cicero *Sententiae Selectae* and *Sententiae Ratae*, "Selected Sayings" and "Authoritative Sayings"). This collection, which is cited in antiquity as the actual work of Epicurus himself rather than as a collection made by his followers, was intended to furnish a practical guide for everyday living. Parallels with the *Letter to Menoeceus* are naturally many, and no effort will be made to call attention to them in the notes.

The text of a number of these *Doctrines* is very bad. I have usually followed Bailey here as elsewhere, but I have made no effort to indicate the rather frequent departures from his text.

The traditional numbering of the *Doctrines* is given in Roman numerals; the figures in the margin are the sections of Laertius' *Life*.

Note *b*, p. 62. No sensation may be rejected, since it truly represents the emanation that has reached us. If the emanation is clear, comes from close at hand, and is repeated without alteration, the concept resulting from the sensation may be accepted as established. If the emanation is isolated or for any reason indistinct, the concept must await confirmation, but the sensation is still evidence that must be considered and must play a part in combination with other evidence in confirming a concept. Thus, every sensation has value and none may be rejected. So, too, the mental examination of an established concept gives valid evidence. In contrast, the examination of a concept awaiting confirmation gives rise only to conjecture of no value for confirming this concept or any other. The first part of the *Doctrine* emphasizes the need of considering every sensation and of rejecting all conjectures based on concepts awaiting confirmation. The last part points out the difference between concepts that are established and those that await confirmation.

The Vatican Sayings

Note *a*, p. 66. This collection, titled *The Sayings of Epicurus,* was found in 1888 in a fourteenth-century Vatican manuscript which also contained Marcus Aurelius' *Meditations,* Epictetus' *Manual,* and similar works. It was discovered too late to be included in Usener's *Epicurea* and was first published by Usener and Hartel in *Wiener Studien,* 1888, pp. 191 ff. It is also to be found in the editions of Epicurus' works by von der Muehll and by Bailey, the last named containing also a translation and commentary, to both of which I am indebted. We have no information when or by whom the Vatican collection was made. Certain of the *Sayings* are identical with some of the *Principal Doctrines,* and others are quite certainly not by Epicurus. In a few cases, the manuscript is so corrupt that it defies certain translation. I have omitted the *Sayings* already translated in the *Principal Doctrines* (*Vatican Saying* I = *Principal Doctrine* I, II = II, III = IV, V = V, VI = XXXV, VIII = XV, XII = XVII, XIII = XXVII, XX = XXIX, XXII = XIX, XLIX = XII, L = VIII, and LXXII = XIII), those certainly not by Epicurus (X, XXX, XXXVI, and XLVII), and those that appear hopelessly corrupt (LVI, LVII, and LXI).

INDEX TO LUCRETIAN REFERENCES

A list of all passages from Lucretius referred to in the notes on the translations, together with the sections of Epicurus for which they are cited.

Lucretius	Epicurus	Lucretius	Epicurus
416-508	89-90a	1028-90	75b-76a
432-94	90b	1117-19	V.S. XXV
509-33	92		
534-48	73b	BOOK VI	
534-63	89-90a		
564-91	91	96-159	100b
566-69	91	160-63	101-102a
575-76	94-95a	164-72	102b
614-49	114a	173-218	101-102a
650-79	92	219-422	103b-104a
680-704	98a	343-44	47b
705-50	94-96a	423-50	104b-105a
751-70	79	451-526	99b-100a
751-70	96b-97	524-26	109b-110a
925-1457	75a-76a	535-607	105b-106a
1010-27	P.D. XXXI	639-702	106b
1010-27	P.D. XXXVI	680-93	106b
		999-1041	62

GENERAL INDEX